Horace Andrew Wadsworth

Quarter-Centennial History of Lawrence, Massachusetts

With Portraits and Biographical Sketches

Horace Andrew Wadsworth

Quarter-Centennial History of Lawrence, Massachusetts
With Portraits and Biographical Sketches

ISBN/EAN: 9783744692588

Printed in Europe, USA, Canada, Australia, Japan

Cover: Foto ©ninafisch / pixelio.de

More available books at **www.hansebooks.com**

QUARTER-CENTENNIAL

HISTORY

—OF—

LAWRENCE, MASSACHUSETTS,

—WITH—

PORTRAITS AND BIOGRAPHICAL SKETCHES

—OF—

EX-MAYORS, THE BOARD OF MAYOR AND ALDERMEN FOR THE PRESENT YEAR, OTHER LEADING OFFICIALS, AND A REPRESENTATION OF BUSINESS AND PROFESSIONAL MEN.

COMPILED BY H. A. WADSWORTH.

PUBLISHED AND PRINTED BY
HAMMON REED; LAWRENCE EAGLE STEAM JOB PRINTING OFFICE.
1878.

PREFATORY.

In the preparation of this work, the author has sought to picture a fleeting phase of our city's life. And let it be remembered that every point of time, each year, each month, each passing moment, marks some era begun, some event completed.

In the history of our city we this year pass the mile stone which marks the quarter of a century. The motto is: "Go forward," but in doing so it is always well, at important turning points, to take a retrospective view, for there is much to be gained for the future through the experiences of the past.

A history is a record of deeds completed, but this book is not wholly that; it is something more. It is a record book of the present. The student of the next century will conceive the active men of to-day, in connection with our city's history, as contemporaneous with those who were indeed the pioneers of our vast manufacturing enterprises. A record of to-day is but the record of our birth; and it is fitting, it is well, before those who were first upon the scene shall have passed away, to put in tangible form for preservation, as near as possible their personal appearance, the battles they fought, and the victories they won in the van of progress and material growth.

The idea of showing by portrait so many familiar faces is somewhat novel, but is one that has been heartily endorsed by a large number of worthy and esteemed citizens. The portraits represent no particular class. The men of the finest broadcloth were not especially sought. They honestly delineate all classes, and are a noble representation of the men who are furnishing the brains and muscle which make our city what it is.

For the historical portion of the book no literary merit is claimed. A book form was adopted so as to put into the hands of the people many facts which were gleaned for publication in the *Essex Weekly Eagle*, in order that they might be better preserved. A newspaper, at best, in a few years grows yellow and illegible, while a book, with good usage, will last for generations. To what was thus published much has been added, although the limited time spent in its compilation has admitted of but a recital of the more important events.

In the preparation much freedom has been used in copying from a short history of Methuen, published in 1876, by Hon. JOSEPH S. HOWE, and also from the history of Andover compiled by ABIEL ABBOT, A. M., in 1829. Besides these, the book on "*The Merrimack River and its Tributaries*," by J. W. MEADER, and published by B. B. Russell, Boston, 1872, has proved a valuable auxiliary for information. And some passages that are quoted are couched in as beautiful and impressive language as pen could indite. To some of our citizens, whose names are mentioned further on, we extend sincere thanks for invaluable aid and assistance.

That perfect accuracy will be found we do not claim. "To err is human," but we have sought accuracy in the aggregate and in detail.

Much has been left unsaid in connection with our young and growing city that deserves a place in history. It is hoped that the OLD RESIDENTS' ASSOCIATION, which, though young in organization, has already collected much valuable historic material, will ere long employ a compiler, and give to us and to posterity a work complete in the fullest detail. With all its imperfections our effort is submitted to the charitable consideration of the public, with the hope that what has been done, regardless of what has been omitted, will be kindly received.

HISTORY.

I.

GEOGRAPHY AND TOPOGRAPHY.

The city of Lawrence is the sixth city in population in the State of Massachusetts. In the year 1875 there were 34,916, and it is safe to presume that at the present writing, (1878) were a census taken, it would show in excess of 38,000 persons. It lies in latitude 42 degrees, 42 minutes, 57.67 seconds, longitude 71 degrees, 9 minutes, 5.85 seconds west from Greenwich. Situated on the Merrimack River, twenty-six miles from its mouth, and is bounded as follows: North, by Methuen; East, by North Andover; South, by Andover; West, by Andover and Methuen. Its area is 4,185 acres, of which 2,173 acres are situated on the north side, and 2012 acres on the south side of the river. It is twenty-six miles north from Boston; ten miles northeast from Lowell, and eight miles west from Haverhill. The Spicket River crosses the northern portion of the city and falls into the Merrimack within the city limits, while the Shawsheen, another important tributary, forms a portion of the southeast boundary, and unites its waters with the Merrimack in the town of North Andover. So much of the city as lies on the north side of the Merrimack River, was formerly a part of the town of Methuen, and that on the south side was formerly a part of Andover.

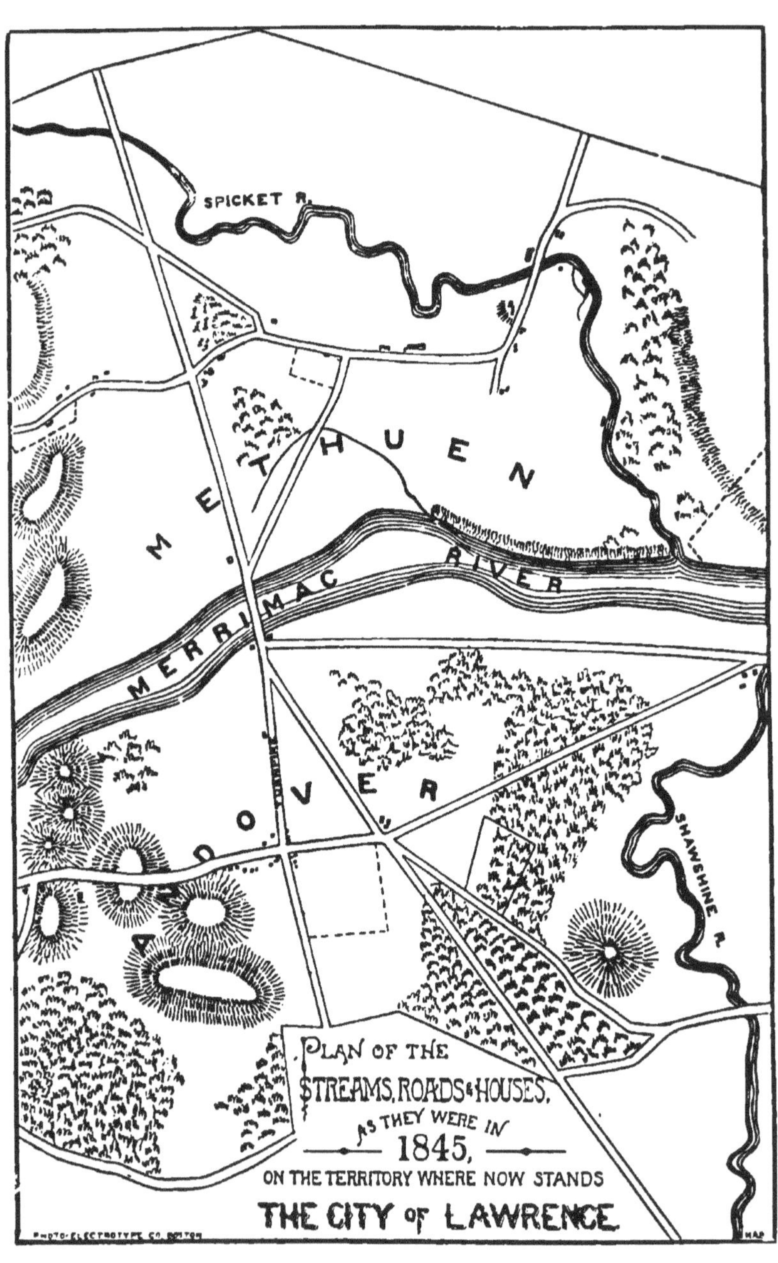
SPICKET R.
METHUEN
MERRIMAC RIVER
ANDOVER
SHAWSHINE R.
PLAN OF THE
STREAMS, ROADS & HOUSES,
AS THEY WERE IN
1845,
ON THE TERRITORY WHERE NOW STANDS
THE CITY OF LAWRENCE
PHOTO-ELECTROTYPE CO. BOSTON

The town of Lawrence was created by an Act of the Legislature, approved March 20, 1845, as follows:

SECT. 1. All the territory now within the towns of Methuen and Andover, in the county of Essex, comprised within the following limits—that is to say, by a line beginning at the mouth of Shawsheen River, at its easterly bank, thence running southerly by said easterly bank to a stake at the bend in said river, a few rods westerly of the bridge, where it is crossed by the Salem Turnpike; thence in a straight line westerly to a marked stone in the wall at the easterly corner of the intersection of roads, by Jacob Barnard's house; thence northerly in a straight line across Merrimack River, passing between the house of Asa Barker and that of Ebenezer Barker, on the Tower-Hill Road, leading from Methuen to Lowell, to a stake about 2,150 feet northerly from where the line crosses said road; thence north-easterly to a monument on the easterly side of Londonderry Turnpike, passing a line northerly of the house of Abiel Stevens; thence easterly in a straight line to a monument at the intersection of Lawrence street with the old road which runs easterly from Stevens' factory towards Haverhill; thence in a straight line easterly, passing north of William Swan's house through a monument about 400 feet south of the intersection of the roads near said Swan's house, to the line of the town of Andover, in Merrimack River; thence running by the said line of Andover westerly, to the easterly bank of Shawsheen River, at the point of starting;—is hereby incorporated into a town by the name of Lawrence: and the said town of Lawrence is hereby invested with all the privileges, powers, rights and immunities, and subject to all the duties and requisitions to which other towns are entitled and subject, by the constitution and laws of this Commonwealth.

SECT. 2. The town of Lawrence shall make and maintain all bridges for public highways over the Shawsheen River, so far as the easterly bank of said river is a boundary of the said town, including the masonry of said bridges on the easterly bank thereof.

SECT. 3. The inhabitants of the said town of Lawrence shall be holden to pay all arrears of taxes which have been legally assessed upon them by the towns of Methuen and Andover, respectively; and all taxes heretofore assessed and not collected, shall be collected and paid to the treasurers of the towns of Methuen and Andover, respectively; in the same manner as if this act had not been passed; and also their proportion of county and state taxes that may be assessed upon them previously to the next state valuation—that is to say, two-thirds of the state and county taxes that may be assessed upon the town of Methuen, and one-eighth of the state and county taxes that may be assessed on the town of Andover, till the next state valuation.

SECT. 4. The parts of the said town of Lawrence now belonging to the towns of Methuen and Andover for the purpose of electing state officers, senators, representatives to congress, and electors of president and vice president of the United States, until the next decennial census shall be taken, in pursuance of the 13th article of amendment to the constitution; and the meetings for the choice of such representatives, and the other officers aforesaid, shall be called by the selectmen of the said towns, respectively; the selectmen of Lawrence shall make a true list of persons belonging to the territory of each of said towns hereby incorporated into the town of Lawrence, qualified to vote at every such election, and the same shall be taken and used by the selectmen of said respective towns for such elections, in the same manner as if prepared by themselves.

SECT. 5. The said towns of Methuen, Andover and Lawrence shall be respectively liable for the support of all who now do, or shall hereafter, stand in need of relief as paupers, whose settlement was gained by, or derived from, a residence within their respective limits; and the said town of Lawrence shall, within one year from the time of its organization under this act pay to the town of Methuen one thousand dollars as and for their just proportion of the debts of the town of Methuen, owing at the time of the passage of this act, exclusive of the amount of the surplus revenue of the United States in the treasury of the town of Methuen; and the town of Lawrence shall also pay two-thirds of the amount of said surplus revenue whenever its repayment shall be demanded by the United States according to law; and shall also pay to the town of Methuen the amount that said town shall pay for building Haverhill street, so called, within the limits of said town of Lawrence, as ordered by the county commissioners for the county of Essex.

SECT. 6 Any justice of the peace in the county of Essex is hereby authorized to issue his warrant directed to any principal inhabitant of the town of Lawrence, requiring him to notify and warn the inhabitants thereof, qualified to vote in town affairs to meet at the time and place appointed, for the purpose of choosing all such town officers as towns are by law authorized and required to choose at their annual meetings; and such justice, or, in his absence, such principal inhabitant shall preside till the choice of a moderator in said meeting.

SECT. 7. This act shall take effect from and after its passage.

Shortly after this act went into effect the necessary steps were taken to give it force, and on the 27th of April, 1847, the new town was ushered in, and officers elected to discharge the duties of the same, as provided by law. The rapid increase of population soon demanded further legislation, and in the year 1853, May 10th, the voters of the then town of Lawrence accepted and put in force a city charter, which, with slight changes, remains the same to the present time.

II.

THE MERRIMACK RIVER.

The Merrimack River from its source to the sea has a fall of something over 5,000 feet. It affords therefore a vast system of mill powers, and gives aid to many kinds of industries, the chief being the manufacture of cotton and woolen fabrics. The amount of manufacturing along this river is not equalled by that upon any other stream in the world. The Merrimack River was known and appreciated far and wide by the aborigines long before the white man bridled and harnessed its majestic falls. Nor is it to be wondered that they prized the numerous advantages it afforded. Capt. John Smith is given credit as being its discoverer, but it appears that DeChamplain, a French navigator, on the seventeenth of July 1605, with a crew of twenty sailors and several French gentlemen were first to enter the bay near where Newburyport now stands, and were therefore really the discoverers of the river. No permanent settlement was made, however, until about twenty years subsequent to this.

The Merrimack River has its source far up in the White Mountain region. The head waters are known as the eastern, western and middle branches, which unite in the town of Woodstock, N. H. The eastern branch is the largest, extending back from this place nearly fifty miles. Few people have undertaken to explore its head waters, and indeed they have their beginning in a wilderness of mountains and forests very little frequented. A score of important tributaries find their way into it in its flow to the sea, several of which have a history of their own of no mean significance. How long the Merrimack River has flowed substantially in its present channel to the sea, of course it is impossible to conjecture. J. W. Meader, in his book on the "Merrimack River," says: "Certain it is, that at some period, far in the dim, distant past, the river was one continuous chain of lakes, whose barriers being worn by water, ice, and drifting wood, have successively given way, until this whole system of collected waters was drained and ultimately reduced to and confined within its present banks. Extensive alluvial deposits indicate the former character of these waters, and their location and dimensions can still be distinctly traced, while far below the surface are found well-defined vegetable deposits, logs and other foreign matter brought here and left, perhaps for evidence of these facts, far away from the present channel of the river. If more proof were needed, it is supplied by the peculiar stratification of the soil, which is regarded by scientific men and geologists as conclusive on this point." But when the Merrimack first occupied the river bed substantially as at present, geologists do not attempt to say.

Far beyond the memory of man or historic date, the Indians held full sway upon its banks, but civilization at last found a foothold here. The first partial survey of the Merrimack River, disclosing its inestimable value and importance for manufacturing purposes, it may, perhaps, be said cast the die. From this time forth the red man made his compulsory bow to the inexorable logic of events, and facing westward with steady advance,—his speed frequently accelerated by the uncomfortable and dangerous proximity of the white man, his last remaining hope to reach the land of the sunset,—he left this river and this land, the home of his boyhood and his manhood, his only patrimony, and the sacred resting place of ancestral dust. It was useless for him to struggle against the decree of fate; and so he left all of these, and the sceptre of his wilderness empire fell from his grasp, his crown tumbled, his ancient power and hereditary rule and supreme kingly prerogatives were stripped from him, and he was sent forth a beggar, an outcast and a vagabond, to be a stranger in a strange land. Thus departed the aboriginal proprietor, and the march of intellect, enterprise, skill, industry and progress supplanted him.

With the white man came cultivation and improvement. The vigorous stroke of the woodman's axe resounded through the forests, roads were made, the log-house and the school-house sprung into existence almost together, the little church reared its tapering spire, as if pointing out to sinful man the way to heaven, to God. The sawmill creaked and grated in harsh, unmusical cadence in many localities along the lesser tributaries of the Merrimack. Hamlets grew to villages, villages to towns and towns to cities. Skill, labor and capital, that all-powerful triumvirate, united their fortunes and interests for the mutual benefit of all. The pioneers pushed steadily up the river, transforming nature's bounties into wealth on every hand. Even the rough uninviting localities at length became the most fruitful vineyards. Enterprises sprung up involving the employment of millions of capital and thousands of people, as if by magic. Every valley and hill within the radius of this river's salutary influence produced its complement of beautiful and noble women, as well as great, good and brave men; and this river gave to the manufacturers along its course an opulence of fame for the unequalled variety, quality and value of their products, which is the property and just pride of the nation.

III
THE INDIANS.

The Indians at the time of their discovery by the Europeans were a race different from any people then known. They were wandering everywhere through the length and breadth of the country. No accurate statement can be given of their numbers, though the best authenticated accounts compute the number in New England at the time of the settlement in Jamestown, Va., 1607, at 123,000, but in the winter of 1617, three years before the landing of the Pilgrims, the plague or some other mortal disease, broke out among them and almost depopulated the country. When the Pilgrims landed in 1620, they saw but few Indians for some days and they were flying from them. Greatly to their comfort and convenience they found deserted wigwams and some corn, which was in good demand among the immigrants. The plague that had two or three years previous depopulated the country seems to have been providential to the early settlers. The number of Indians however left scattered about in what is now Massachusetts was not much less than 10,000 or 12,000. In Rhode Island about 8,000 and in New Hampshire about 4,000. The whole number of warriors in New England is estimated at 12,000 at the time of the arrival of our ancestors. The features of these New England Indians were good, especially those of the women; their hair bright and straight, their limbs clean, straight, and well proportioned. They were quite ingenious in their way; were quick of apprehension; sudden in despatch; subtle in their dealings; ready in invention, and in labor assiduous. They had wigwams, or cabins, to protect them from the weather. These were built by uniting poles at the top, and inserting them in the ground at suitable distance. These were covered with bark, boughs of trees, or skins except an aperture at the top for smoke, and a small place for entrance at the sides. The fire was built in the centre; the ground around the fire was covered with mats, skins or boughs, as they could afford. They used no chairs, but sat on this covering, and had no need for a table. They slept with their feet towards the fire. A whole family, and sometimes more, were accommodated in one of these cabins, which had but one room. They were commonly located near good water. They had skins for clothing when the English came among them, from which they made moccasins for their feet. They often caught fish with a kind of spear. They used bows and arrows for hunting and for defence. The end of the arrow was pointed with flint stone. These points have been frequently found in the fields in this vicinity long since the Indians departed. They made canoes of bark taken from large birch trees. This was sewed together with fibres or roots. It was put in proper shape and strengthened by ribs or thin pieces of wood, and a rim, like the top of a basket, was fastened all around it and bound with tough bark or fibres of roots. It was daubed with pitch to prevent leaking. With these canoes they could pass up and down or across the rivers, and they were large enough to carry several persons. They were light and might be carried with ease around water falls, or from one stream to another.

The Merrimack River, (Called Menomack by the Indians, from Mena, an island, and awke, a place, from the number of beautiful islands in the river), furnished a locality greatly admired by the Indians. They were certainly great admirers of the beautiful and grand in nature, and the numerously settled localities and names of tribes upon the river and its tributaries, give incontestible proof of this. "As the artisan, mechanic, manufacturer and capitalist of modern times learned the adaptation and capacity of this river as a motive power and congregated about its falls,—constructing dams to catch the water on its journey down, erecting monster mills with massive six-story brick walls, building populous cities and beautiful villages, fabricating unsurpassed cotton and woolen goods, machinery and implements,— so did the red man of primitive days learn the peculiar fitness of this river for supplying his necessities and wants, equally as pressing and urgent as those of his more civilized successors." Along the banks of the river in this vicinity especially on the Andover side was a favorable resort for their mode of life. There was plenty of fish in the river and numerous streams running into it; the light land near the water was suitable for the cultivation of corn and beans, and the forests afforded abundant game. In the fishing season the Indians caught a great many fish by a sort of scoop net; only the salmon were kept for food while the remainder were used for manure on the land. It was a festival season with them; the squaws preparing fish for the repast, for preservation, and for barter, while the night was passed in feasting and dancing. At these fishing-seasons, lovers' vows were plighted, marriages were consummated, speeches made and treaties formed. Particular periods and important events were noted and celebrated among them with great ceremony. Among the established institutions or customs may be mentioned the Recruiting, or Fire Brand Dance. When the declaration of war had been announced by the chief, a great fire was built of brushwood, pine knots, and sticks near the wigwam, and—

By the red sun's parting glance,
They gathered for the warrior's dance:
First in a circle wide they stand,
Each with an arrow in his hand;
Then crouching, and with bended bow,
They step to measure light and slow;
Now quicker with a savage flurry,
They circle round and hurry, hurry,
Now the ring breaks, and leaping, yelling,
In one discordant chorus swelling;
Then tomahawks are brandished high;
Their shouts re-echo from the sky;
Their blood stained nostrils opened wide,
Their foaming lips all dark and gory,
Make up the red man's scene of glory.—*Stark.*

At the time of the first settlements on the Merrimack River, the most powerful and important tribe along its banks were the Pennacooks. Their headquarters were on the river near where Concord, New Hampshire, is now built. Their great chief was Passaconnaway. He had conquered and subdued all the tribes on the river, and all in some manner paid tribute to him. The Agawams inhabited the river East below tide water, having their homes from the Merrimack to the Cape. The Pentuckets owned and occupied the Merrimack from "Little River" in Haverhill to Pawtucket Falls at Lowell, then came the Wamesits, Nashua, Souhegan, Namoskeag, Winnipesaukee, and several other tribes. There is no evidence showing that any particular tribe had a home in Methuen, but it is certain that Bodwells Falls, now Lawrence dam, and the shores of the Spicket were favorite resorts, especially in the fishing season. On the Andover side, a company of the Pentuckets with a chief known as Roger, had a settlement near Cochickewick Brook. Some writers have located the ancient seat of the Agawams at Bodwells Falls, and at this place came to reside the Princess of the House of Pennacook, the daughter of Passaconnaway, who was wedded to Winnepurket, a sachem of Saugus. "The Poet of the Merrimack" has commemorated this event by a poem in which he characterizes the groom as the "dog of the marshes." The union was not a happy one, and an estrangement soon sprung up which came near resulting in war, and likely would, had not the "pale faces" appeared upon the stage about this time.

As has been above stated, the great warrior and chieftain of the Merrimack at the time of the first settlement was Passaconnaway, whose home was well up the head waters of the river. He was a friend to the white settlers and desired peace, and the residents along the river were never disturbed by Indian depredations during his life. He resigned his power as Grand Sachem of the tribes in 1660 to Wonolancet, about twenty years after the first white settlements upon the river. His successor afterwards became converted to christianity by the great Indian missionary Eliot, but notwithstanding this, he and his tribe received most cruel and inhuman treatment at the hands of the approaching settlers. The farewell address of Passaconnaway, who lived to be over 80 years old, well conveys to the reader of to-day the feelings that inspired the breasts of the aborigines. On a given day, he called around him the leading warriors, chiefs and principals of his tribes and thus addressed them :—

"Hearken to the words of your father. I am an old oak that has withstood the storms of more than a hundred winters. Leaves and branches have been stripped from me by winds and frosts; my eyes are dim—my limbs totter—I must soon fall. But when young and sturdy, when my bow—no young man of the Pennacooks could bend it; when my arrows would pierce a deer at a hundred yards, and I could bury my hatchet in a sapling to the eye, no wigwam had so many furs, no pole so many scalps as Passaconnaway's. Then I delighted in war. The whoop of the Pennacooks was heard upon the Mohawk, and no voice so loud as Passaconnaway's. The scalps upon my pole in the wigwam told the story of Mohawk suffering. The English came, they seized our lands. I sat me down at Pennacook. They followed upon my footsteps. I made war upon them, but they fought me with fire and thunder; my young men were swept down before me when no one was near them. I tried sorcery against them; but they still increased, and prevailed over me and mine, and I gave place to them and retired to my beautiful island of Natticook. I that can make the dry leaf turn green and live again,—I that can take the rattlesnake in my palm as I would a worm, without harm,—I, who had communication with the Great Spirit, dreaming and awake,—I am powerless before the pale-faces. The oak will soon break before the whirlwind; it shivers and shakes even now; soon its trunk will be prostrate; the ant and the worm will sport upon it! Then think, my children of what I say. I commune with the Great Spirit. He whispers me now :—

"'Tell your people, peace, peace is the only hope of your race. I have given fire and thunder to the pale-faces for weapons. I have made them plentier than the leaves of the forest, and still shall they increase! These meadows they shall turn with the plow; these forests shall fall by the axe; the pale-faces shall live upon your hunting grounds, and make their villages upon your fishing-places.' The Great Spirit says this, and it must be so! We are few and powerless before them! We must bend before the storm! The wind blows hard! The old oak trembles! Its branches are gone! Its sap is frozen! It bends! It falls! Peace, peace with the white men, is the command of the Great Spirit, and the wish—the last wish—of Passaconnaway."

IV.

EARLY SETTLERS.

In the year 1640 eight men belonging to the colony at Newbury, named William White, Samuel Gile, James Davis, Henry Palmer, John Robinson, Christopher Massey, John Williams and Richard Littlehale, together with four men from the Ipswich settlement, named Abraham Tyler, Daniel Ladd, Joseph Merrie and Jacob Clement being "straitened" for tillage and grass land, proceeded up the Merrimack River as far as "Little River," a tributary, that rises in Plaistow and empties into the Merrimack a few miles below Mitchell's Falls. Here they founded a settlement and called it Haverhill. They adopted the same course towards the Indians as did other New England settlers—that of purchasing of the rightful owners, as near as could be ascertained, the land they wished to occupy. A few of the remnants of the Pentucket tribe were scattered about this locality. The settlers sought out their chiefs, and two years after, the following deed was drawn, signed and acknowledged, which is now in possession of the city of Haverhill:

"KNOW ALL MEN BY THESE PRESENTS, that we Passaquo and Saggahew, with ye consent of Passaçonnaway, have sold unto ye inhabitants of Pentuckett all ye lands we have in Pentuckett; that is eyght myles in length from ye little Rivver in Pentuckett Westward; Six myles in length from ye aforesaid Rivver northward; And six myles in length from ye aforesaid Rivver Eastward, with ye Ileand and ye rivver that ye ileand stand in as far in length as ye land lyes by as formerly expressed; that is fourteen myles in length;

And wee ye said Passaquo and Sagga Hew, with ye consent of Passaconnaway, have sold unto ye said inhabitants all ye right wee or any of us have in ye said ground and Ileand and Rivver;

And we warrant it against all or any other Indians whatsoever unto ye said Inhabitants of Pentuckett, and to their heirs and assigns forever. Dated ye fifteenth day of november Ann Dom 1642.

Witness our hands and seales to this bargayne of sale ye day and year above writted (in ye presents of us) we ye said Passaquo and Sagga Hew have received in hand, for & in consideration of ye same three pounds & ten shillings.

JOHN WARD,
ROBERT CLEMENTS,
TRISTRAM COFFIN,
HUGH SHERRATT,
WILLIAM WHITE,
ye sign of (1)
THOMAS DAVIS.

YE MARKE OF
PASSAQUO (a bow and arrow)
PASSAQUO. [SEAL.]

YE MARKE OF
SAGGA HEW (a bow and arrow)
SAGGA HEW. [SEAL."

It is impossible to determine with any degree of definiteness the boundaries of the territory intended to be conveyed by this deed, nor is it to be supposed that the purchasers cared much, except that they got possession of the land on the Merrimack for a dozen miles. More than twenty years elapsed before any survey was attempted. In the year 1666 the General Court appointed a committee to "run the bounds of the town of Haverhill." They began at the meeting-house, which was situated about a half-mile east of Little River, and ran due west eight miles and reared "a heap of stones," which point must be a little west of Salem Village. They then ran from that point due south till they struck the Merrimack River near Pine Island, a little way from the Bartlett Farm, three miles above this city. Thence northeasterly by the river, till they reached the point of beginning. The land on the northwest, between Methuen and Dracut, a strip about a mile and a half wide, was deeded by the General Court to individuals.

ISAAC TEWKSBURY,

Physician and Surgeon ; office and residence, 295 Essex Street. Born at West Newbury, Jan. 13, 1795 ; brought up on a farm and educated at Atkinson Academy and Hebron Academy, Oxford, Me. Was clerk in stores and offices at Newburyport, Portland and New York for a short time, then studied medicine with Drs. Robinson of Newbury, Tewksbury of Hebron, Maine, Little of Gloucester, Me., and Kittredge of Andover. Commenced practice at Hampstead, N. H., 1817, remaining 30 years in practice without vacation or sickness. Came to Lawrence in 1847. Married Sabra Foster, at Hudson, N. H., 1822, and Widow Harriet W. Smith, Lawrence, for his second wife, 1859 ; has six children. Is a member of the Congregational church, Hampstead. Dr. Tewksbury is the oldest man in active business in Lawrence and has been in the continuous practice of his profession sixty-one years.

*The uplands at that time were mostly covered by a heavy growth of timber, except an occasional spot burned over by fires set by the Indians. The meadows were, many of them, cleared and covered with a tall dense growth of grass. The Indians were accustomed to burn the grass in the fall, that they might more easily capture the deer resorting to them to feed upon the young grass in the spring. These meadows appear to have been much sought after by the early settlers, who obtained from them the principal subsistence for their cattle. They cut and stacked the hay in the summer, and in winter drew it home on sleds. An early writer says of Haverhill: "The people were wholly bent to improve their labor in tilling the earth and keeping of cattle, whose yearly increase encourages them to spend their days in those remote parts. The constant penetrating into this wilderness hath caused the wild and uncouth wood to be filled with frequented ways, and the large rivers to be overlaid with bridges passable both for horse and foot; this town is of large extent, there being an overweaning desire in most men after meadow land," &c. The records of the town of Haverhill show that no one was admitted to the rights and privileges of the colony unless first voted in by the town.

The lands were divided among the inhabitants in accordance with a vote "That he who had £200 should have twenty acres for his house lot, and every one under that sum to have ten acres proportioned for his house lot, together with meadow and common and planting ground proportionately."

Lot-layers were chosen by the town to divide the land among the inhabitants as it was cleared up or became accessible. From this mode of division it happened that one man would own a number of small lots scattered over the whole town. It is now very difficult to exactly locate the lots as they are recorded in the Haverhill records, because they were usually bounded only by marked trees. These descriptions show that some of our local names were of very ancient date. In

* Howe's History of Methuen.

1673, thirty-two acres of land were laid off to John Clements, bounded by "Sowe's Brook." In 1678, "eleven score acres of upland" were laid off to James Davis, Sen., bounded on the west by Spicket River, Spicket Falls being the southwest bound. In 1683, there is a record of a similar lot lying on the southerly side, running to "Bloody Brook on the east, and taken up by James Davis, Jr. These lots included the land now occupied by the east part of Methuen village.

In 1658 five acres of meadow were laid off in "Strongwater," near a "little pond." In 1666 a parcel of meadow was laid out to Matthias Button, on the south side of "Spicket Hill." In 1659 there was a division of the land west of the Spicket River, with a provision that "if more than two acres meadow be found in any one lot it shall remain to the town. In the same year there is a record of the laying off three acres of land in "Mistake Meadow" in the west part of Haverhill, whence it is concluded the name originated in somebody's blunder, and has become "Mystic." The distribution of common lands was continued from time to time, until finally, after much contention between the old settlers and new comers, the "Proprietors," or owners of the common land, organized separately from the town and disposed of the remaining land as they saw fit. David Nevins, Esq., of Methuen, has in his possession a grant from the "proprietors," of the islands in the Spicket above the falls, to Asa and Robert Swan, for £2 10*s*., and bearing the date of 1721.

No record can be found showing when the first settlement was made within the limits of Methuen, or who made it. It is certain that the east and south parts of the town, near the river, were first occupied, doubtless because they were nearer the villages of Haverhill and Andover. It is stated by Asa Simonds, Esq., that when repairing the old "Bodwell house"—now in Lawrence—some years ago, a brick was found bearing the date 1660, which had been marked upon it

ARTEMAS W. STEARNS,

Dry Goods Dealer, 309 Essex St., the first dry goods dealer in the city. Residence, No. 7 Lowell Street. He came to Lawrence in 1846, from Methuen. Born at Hill, N. H., 1816. Educated at academies in New Market and Nashua. Mr. Stearns had a store in a brick block on Amesbury St., two years; on Merchants' Row, three years; where Taylor & Dow now occupy, three years. Built his present store in 1853; enlarged in 1877–8. Mr. Stearns has the largest dry goods store in the county; employs 75 hands in its various departments. He has also a farm of 60 acres on Lawrence St. Is president of the Lawrence National Bank; treasurer of the Wright Manuf'g Co.; director and heaviest stockholder in the M. V. H. R. R., trustee Broadway Savings Bank, and member board of investment. Married Lydia Searles of Nashua, N. H.; no children. Attends Central Congregational Church.

before the brick was burnt. This would seem to indicate that a house was built in the neighborhood near that date.

It is not unlikely that further inquiry may fix the date and place of the first settlement here with considerable certainty. It seems doubtful whether there were many settlers in Methuen until near the time it was set off from Haverhill. It is likely that the Indian troubles which extended over many years previous to 1700, seriously checked, if they did not entirely prevent, the settlement on farms. Andover and Haverhill were made frontier towns by act of General Court, and both towns suffered severely during the Indian war. But there is no record of any Indian attack upon settlers living upon territory which afterwards became Methuen. There were many attacks on the scattered settlers in West Haverhill and in Andover, and if there had been many inhabitants in Methuen, it is hardly probable that the Indians would have passed them by.

In 1722, a petition was presented to the town of Haverhill by persons living in what is now Methuen, to be set off as a separate town or parish. This petition was not granted. The next year Joshua Swan and 26 others, with shrewd foresight, petitioned the town of Haverhill to "set off fifty or sixty acres of land southwest of Bare Meadow, together with a piece of land lying on a hill commonly called Meeting House Hill in times past, reserved by our forefathers for the use of the ministry, might in hard times make a convenient parsonage, if by the blessing of God the gospel might so flourish amongst us, and we grow so prosperous as to be able to maintain and carry on the gospel ministry amongst us." This petition was granted at the next town meeting, but it did not serve to make the petitioners less intent upon a separation. Soon after, Lieut. Stephen Barker and other inhabitants of the western part of Haverhill, petitioned the General Court for an act to incorporate them into a new town. The act passed in December, 1725, and was soon carried into effect.

Unfortunately at the outset, a bitter quarrel sprang up concerning the location of the meeting-house. On the 28th of May, 1726, a meeting was called to "prefix" a place whereon to build a meeting-house. Twenty-eight persons voted in favor of locating the house "between James Davis's and Samuel Smith's house" (Powder House Hill,) twenty-two entered their "dissent against the meeting-house being carried from the meeting-house land or hill, so called,"—the land which had been granted by Haverhill two years before—and supported their "dissent" by a quaint and vigorous argument. The dispute waxed hot, meeting after meeting was held, votes to provide labor and material were carried and reconsidered, but the majority finally prevailed and the new meeting-house was raised and boarded on "Powder House hill." The minority, however, were determined not to be beaten, and petitioned the General Court to reverse the popular decision. The committee appointed by the Court to visit the place concluded that the parsonage lot 'was the properest place for the meeting-house to stand,' so the minority were victorious, and in May, 1727, the town voted to remove the frame to the place where the Court ordered it should stand.

The town records show that the Sunday services, as well as the town meetings, were held at the house of Asie Swan until the meeting house was ready for occupancy. Asie Swan seems to have been a man 'prominent in those days,' and his house is said to have been situated a little east of Prospect hill. The meeting-house was "forty feet long, thirty feet wide, and twenty feet stud." There was but one pew, and that for the minister's family, the congregation generally being seated on benches. There were no means of heating the house in cold weather, until within the recollection of persons now living, and in the cold winter mornings the humble worshipers must have needed a fiery discourse to make them comfortable. It is said that there was a tavern in those days on the "Frye place" to which the meeting goers usually resorted at noon, where they found a kettle of

JAMES DAY HERRICK,

Boot and Shoe Merchant, 139 Essex St. Residence, 356 Haverhill St., corner of Franklin St. Has been a resident of Lawrence from its organization. Was born in Derry, N. H., April 20, 1810. Worked on his father's farm until nineteen years of age. Attended school at South Reading, Phillips Academy at Andover, and Dartmouth College, Hanover, N. H., five years and one half. Taught district school until 1846, when he commenced taking toll at the Andover bridge. Married Miss Louisa Robinson May 17, 1848, and continued in the employ of the Andover Bridge Co. twenty-two years, during which time he was frequently elected to the most responsible offices in the gift of the city: Chief of Police, City Assessor, Chief Engineer of the Fire Department, member of the Board of Aldermen, but oftener as one of the Board of School Committee.

hot water ready, and plenty of *spiritual* comfort less etherial than that which they received within the sacred edifice.

The first road laid out by the Town of Methuen extended from somewhere on "Hawkes Meadow brook to James Howe's well," and was probably a part of Howe Street north of the Taylor farm. The records of the town of Haverhill show that previous to that time a large number of town ways had been laid out in the west part of the town—probably for convenience in reaching the meadows and woodland.

The roads of those days were probably little better than an ordinary cart path in the woods. Occasionally may be found a record of money paid to the owners of land over which a public way passed, but no money appears to have been paid by the town for building. In fact scarcely more than a path was necessary, for there were no vehicles but ox carts and sleds. People traveled on horseback and went to market with their goods in saddlebags. Indeed it is said by persons now living in this vicinity that within their recollection there were no wagons of any kind, or pleasure carriages except a few chaises, which were introduced about the beginning of the century.

An old tax book among the town records, shows that the number of persons taxed in Methuen in 1740, was 165, of which 71 lived in that part of the town cut off by the New Hampshire line, and 85 in the present limits of Methuen.

The fact that strikes one most forcibly in reading over the early town records, is the prominence given to religious observances. The chief and only reason given for setting off the new town was that the people might more easily attend the public worship of God. The first business done was to provide themselves a minister and place of public worship. Their principal money tax was for support of those objects. Nothing could show more plainly that the hardy pioneers of Methuen were of genuine Puritan stock. Whatever may be thought of Puritan austerity and fanaticism and intolerance, one cannot help admiring the indomitable energy, the iron will, and lofty purpose of those men who braved the dangers of hostile Indians, and suffered the privations of the wilderness, that they might worship God in their own way. The old papers which have been preserved, the town records, and the old traditions all show that the first settlers in Methuen were men of rugged, vigorous intellect, accustomed to think for themselves, and not afraid to express their opinions.

The number of inhabitants in Methuen in 1776, according to the Colonial Census, was 1326. The old tax book of that year gives the names of 252 poll-tax payers. This was at the breaking out of the revolutionary war, and let it be remembered that Methuen at the first call for soldiers to protect themselves against the British, with only 252 poll-tax payers, sent 156 men. They had no opportunity to meet the red coats till the battle of Bunker Hill, at which the Methuen company, under Capt. John Davis, bore an important part.

Up to the year 1793 there were no bridges across the Merrimack River in this vicinity, and ferries furnished the only means of crossing. There were five of these as follows: "Gage's Ferry," near the house of Samuel Cross; "Swan's Ferry," at Wingate's Farm; "Marston's Ferry," at the alms house, Lawrence; "Bodwell's Ferry," at the Lawrence pumping station; "Harris' Ferry," a little east of Dracut line.

The territory now comprising Ward Six, south side of the river, was formerly a part of Andover. The first settlers of this town did not migrate up the Merrimack. In 1634, four years after the first planting of Charlestown and Boston, those of Newtown, now Cambridge, complained of straitness for want of land, and desired leave of the Court to look out for enlargement, or removal, which was granted. They then "Sent men to Merrimack to find a fit place to transplant themselves." In the same year the following order of the Court was passed:

"It is ordered that the land about Cochickewick be reserved for an inland plantation, and whosoever shall go there to inhabit shall

AARON ORDWAY,

Was born at Hebron, N. H., May 4, 1814. Came to Lawrence Mar., 1847, establishing himself in business as an apothecary and in practice as a physician. This business and profession he followed for about twenty-four years. Eight years since he retired from practice, but is active as president and a principal owner and director in Brown's Lumber Co. of Whitefield, N. H. He is also president of the newly organized Whitefield & Jefferson R. R. Co. His father was a hardy pioneer settler of Hebron, N. H., living to the ripe age of 93. His uncle, John Ordway, was clerk and historian of the Lewis and Clark U. S. Exploring Expedition. In early life Dr. Ordway had only the advantages of a common school education, and for several years before coming to Lawrence was engaged in mercantile business, and for three years in the practice of medicine. Alderman in 1857 and 1858. Has been twice married and has four children.

have three years immunity from all taxes, levies, public charges and services whatsoever, military discipline only excepted."

It is difficult to ascertain the time of the first settlement in Andover. The land was purchased of Cutshamache, the Sagamore of Massachusetts, by Mr. Woodbridge, for six pounds and a coat in behalf of the inhabitants. This purchase was confirmed by the Court in 1646. The first settlements were made upon the Cochickewick and Shawsheen. All of the early settlers were born in Great Britain and most of them in England. On a leaf of the town records of Andover the following list is written in ancient hand, without date, but probably when most of the first settlers were living:

"The names of all the householders in order as they came to town: Mr. Bradstreet, John Osgood, Joseph Parker, Richard Barker, John Stevens, Nicholas Holt, Benj. Woodbridge, John Frye, Edmund Faulkner, Robert Barnard, Daniel Poor, Nathan Parker, Henry Jaques, John Aslett, Richard Blake, William Ballard, John Lovejoy, Thomas Poor, George Abbott, John Russ, Andrew Allen, Andrew Foster, Thomas Chandler."

Such portions of land as were necessary for the use of the settlers were, from time to time, set off to individuals in proportion to the expenses or taxes paid by each, and their several divisions recorded in the town book. When a person moved into town for the purpose of settling, land was sold to him by the town and he was received as a commoner, or proprietor. The business was conducted in this manner for more than fifty years. The first divisions were made in small lots, few of them exceeding ten acres plough land, and land not easy of tillage, was granted at a distance on the plains; swamp or meadow land for hay, and woodland often at quite a distance away. This method of laying off farms has rendered them very inconvenient and much inconvenience from this early division remains to this date, very few farms of considerable size being compact.

To show the tastes, temper and disposition of these early settlers a few acts of the town of Andover as put upon record are here given :

" 1660.—The town looking into consideration the great damage that may come to the town by persons living remote upon such lands as were given them for ploughing and planting, and so by their hogs and cattle destroy the meadows adjoining thereunto, have ordered, and do hereby order, that whatsoever inhabitant or other shall build any dwelling house in that part of the town but upon house lots, and other places granted for that end, without express leave from the town shall forfeit 20 shillings a month for the time he shall live on any such prohibited place,—the town having given house lots to build on to all such as they have received as inhabitants of the town.

1664.—Attendance of every voter was required, and every neglect to come to the town meeting at the day and time appointed subjected the delinquent to a forfeiture of 12 pence.

1672.—It is ordered that whatsoever dogs shall be in the meeting house on the Sabbath day, the owner thereof shall pay 6 pence for every time being there, and G. A. Jr., is appointed to take notice thereof and have the pay for his pains and to gather it up.

1680.—It was voted and agreed upon that if any person whether male or female, shall sit in any other place in the meeting house than where they are appointed by the committee shall forfeit for every such offense for the use of the town twenty pence, to be forthwith gathered by the constable by order of said committee and if the constable faileth to do as abovesaid to pay said sum himself.

1689.—Ordered by the selectmen that no persons entertain others in their houses after 9 o'clock in the evening without warrantable business, on penalty of five shillings. No young persons to be abroad on Saturday or Sunday nights, nor people to entertain on these nights in the like penalty,—persons unseasonably away from their own homes exposed to the same forfeiture. The tithingmen were required to examine and report the breaches of these orders.

1695.—Two persons were appointed by the Selectmen to sit in the galleries to inspect the young on the Sabbath and were required to notify disorderly persons to the minister."

The settlers of Andover during these years had much trouble with the Indians. Shortly after Passaconnaway's death in 1660 a war sprung up between the Indians and the whites which was waged at

ASA M. BODWELL,

Farmer,—"to the manor born," living upon the estate of his ancestors, now comprising 190 acres. Mr. Bodwell has sold considerable of the original estate, including the site of the city reservoir, and has also added several parcels. He was born in 1812, and has spent his life upon the old homestead, excepting a few years passed at the west in early manhood; has never married. He received the educational advantages offered by the common schools of this valley fifty years ago. About four years ago he moved the old wooden house of his ancestors and erected the fine brick edifice, No. 589 Haverhill Street, where he now resides.

intervals till the year 1696. Subsequent to this date Andover was not a frontier town, and no depredations by the Indians in this vicinity are reported. During the next century and a quarter the sturdy yeomanry on either side of the river moved on in the even tenor of their way, little dreaming of the changes the next century would produce. After the factories had been set in motion in Lowell, people about here began to wonder whether Bodwell's Falls and other rapids in the river near them could and would ever be utilized. At one time about the year 1825, as Dr. Isaac Tewksbury was riding over Phillips Hill in company with Dr. Kittredge, of North Andover, they halted and took a bird's eye survey of this valley and remarked upon the feasibility and probability of a future city. At that time there were not over 200 persons residing in the territory now comprising the city of Lawrence.

A * writer of the Old Residents' Association says, that no church spire pointed to heaven in this valley; only three school buildings, of limited capacity, with primitive accommodations, stood within present city limits. There was no hum of machinery excepting the simple movements of the small paper and grist mills on the lower Spicket and the activity at Stevens' workshop, on the site of the Arlington Mills. But here was the waterfall, the noble sweep of river, the lesser streams winding their way through wooded valleys to meet the Merrimack. Here were the sandy Shawsheen fields in Andover, long tilled by savage and civilized hands and the sparsely settled farms, with wooded pastures, lying along the north bank of the river in Methuen, with the same rounded hills to eastward and westward. Here was the swell of land, between the Merrimack and Spicket rivers, favoring building, drainage and a regular arrangement of city streets; here were all the possibilities of future activity waiting the advent of men bold, enterprising and skilful enough to transform this sleepiest of rural neighborhoods into a centre of activity and life.

* Hon. R. H. Tewksbury.

The Andover tract was known as the "Moose Country" or the Plain of Sodom, and the chief innkeeper at the Cross roads was familiarly called Lot. The Methuen district was in retaliation called Gomorrah by dwellers on the opposite bank. A ravine traversed by a small intermittent stream bisected this Methuen plain, leaving the river from a point near the Central Pacific Mill, running northerly inland, nearly with the line of Lawrence street, bending westward and broadening into a basin lying between the line of Haverhill street and Amesbury and Franklin streets. This basin, now mostly filled and drained, has become the heart of population in Wards Three and Four.

A gulley or run extending from the Washington Mills, nearly on a line with Jackson street, to the quagmire which formed the easterly part of Lawrence Common. Below Union street, eastward from the Duck Mills, was a sunken valley, lower than the bottom of the canal, requiring a vast amount of filling. There was a shorter ravine where the Atlantic Mills are located, and another low run extending inland, towards depot square, from a point near the counting house of the main Pacific Mills. Depot square and its immediate vicinity was a pool of stagnant water, well stocked with pouts and other fish. A ridge or bluff of bluestone ran parallel with Essex street, to the rear of where the post office now stands, from which, in the early days of the city, cannon were fired in times of jubilation and political rejoicing.

Haverhill and East Haverhill streets follow substantially old county roads, changed somewhat in direction and grade; Broadway is a section of the old turnpike laid out in 1806, from Concord, N. H., to Medford, Mass., that part within the city limits taking the name a few years since. Portions of Cross, Arlington, Berkeley, and Marston streets in North Lawrence, and of Lowell road, Salem turnpike and Merrimack street in South Lawrence, with the ferry and back roads in the outlying wards, follow substantially old thoroughfares.

W. R. SPALDING.

Captain Spalding was born in Wilton, N. H. in 1828. Came to Lawrence in 1846, and entered the clothing business, in which he has from that time been engaged, and is consequently the oldest merchant in the city. He obtained the charter of the Merrimack Valley Horse Railroad, and was largely instrumental in its being built, and was at one time extensively interested in the Concord Railroad, and one of its directors for several years. At the present time he is one of the directors of the Lowell & Lawrence Railroad, and is, under appointment of Gov. Rice, one of the Inspectors of State Charitable Institutions for Paupers and Insane at Tewksbury; is also a director of the Pemberton National Bank and treasurer of the Lawrence Savings Bank. He has served in both branches of the city government. Married Mary A. Ham, a native of Rochester, N. H.

The old ferry roads had much travel before the building of Andover bridge; they compassed the valley, now the site of the city. The westerly road approached from the north, reaching the Merrimack at Bodwell's ferry, near pumping station, by way of Currant, (Bellevue) and Tower Hill, running as now, to the rear of Bellevue Cemetery. The easterly road ran as it now runs, over and a little to the eastward of Prospect Hill, reaching the Merrimack at Marston's ferry, near the Lawrence poor farm, where was also, in the olden time, a ford.

After the building of the Andover Bridge, in 1793, a rough roadway ran from the bridge, northeasterly, across the lowlands to a point just west of the First Baptist church, where it joined the Haverhill road.

The few dwellings dotting the plain within the central wards were mostly upon the road, now straightened, graded and known as Haverhill and East Haverhill streets. On East Haverhill street was and still is the old house, with its immense elm, both now standing, almost the only undisturbed relics of a former century, in the populous districts of the city. A part of this ancient dwelling is so old that it ante-dates all recollections or traditions, excepting the known fact that it once stood near the mouth of the Spicket River, on the Merrimack bank, before roads were opened in the region, and sheltered one of the first settlers on this plain. The great farm belonging with this estate lay along the western bank of the Spicket river, and extended from the Merrimack to the westward bend of the Spicket, and westerly to the Gage farm, hereafter mentioned. The old house was removed to the present site, when highways were laid out, and large additions made thereto. The great elm was transplanted from the Spicket bank by a tramping soldier of the old French war, about one hundred and twenty-six years ago, at the request of the fair wife of the farmer residing there. The estate is now the homestead of W. B. Gallison, Esq. Opposite this ancient landmark was the more modern dwelling of Adolphus Durant, Esq., built a little more than fifty years ago; with a snug enclosure of surrounding land with the buildings. The house is well remembered, and was removed a few years since and fitted for tenants.

The farm house and buildings of the late Phineas M. Gage, stood in the fields on the spot now known as Jackson Terrace; the old well with curb and sweep, was just at the rear of the Unitarian church, the farm orchard was in the section of the city now crossed by Orchard street, his garden extending along the line of Garden street. Thus the names of two city streets are naturally accounted for. The farm of Mr. Gage extended from the banks of the Merrimack to Spicket River, including the eastern end of the common, and the lands eastward to a line near Newbury street.

The substantial dwelling standing upon the site of the high school building is so well remembered as hardly to need mention. It was occupied in old times, in turn by one Remick, a sea-faring man, and one Thwing from Dorchester, and by Daniel Merrill, Esq., later of Methuen. Lawrence common was mostly within the lines of this estate, which included all of the central and westerly portion.

The ancient homestead of Capt. White stood just west of the residence of J. H. Battles, Esq., near the corner of Haverhill and Lawrence streets. His farm lands extended westerly to Cross street and northward to Spicket river, with a large central tract south of Haverhill street. His son Judge Daniel Appleton White, born beneath the old sloping roof, gave the citizens of Lawrence what must continue to prove a source of perpetual pleasure and incalculable profit, his munificent gift for the founding of a course of lectures, established and known as the "White Fund Course," and from the fund material aid is given to sustain and enlarge the public library. The more modest farm house at the corner of Amesbury and Haverhill streets was, with several acres of surrounding lands, the property of Fairfield White, Esq., now living, hale and hearty, a resident of Methuen, and still holding a part of those lands. A substantial square farm house, near where E. W. Colcord now lives, at the corner of Franklin and Haver-

STEPHEN P. SIMMONS,

Stone Contractor and Builder. Residence, 175 Haverhill St. Has been in Lawrence since April 1st, 1847. Was born in Foster, R. I., April 17, 1813. Received a common school education. Learned the mason's trade in 1833, at Woonsocket Falls, R. I. Was married in 1834, in Smithfield, R. I., to Fannie B. Eldridge of South Harwich, Mass.; has four children. Attends the First Methodist church. He helped to build the dam across the Merrimack River, built the stone chimney in Everett yard, Grace Episcopal church, all the foundations, excavating, grading, etc., for Lawrence jail, stone church in Methuen, and re-built the foundation of the Pemberton Mill after its fall. In 1854 did several thousand dollars' worth of work for the Essex Co. Mr. Simmons was present at the organization of the town of Lawrence, and also voted at the first city election.

hill streets, was known at one time as the Sargent house. It was torn down about the time the city was incorporated.

The buildings of the Methuen poor farm, formerly owned by Nathaniel Sargent, stood near the corner of Bradford street and Broadway, then the corner of Haverhill road and old turnpike, and were too lately removed to need special description.

The town farm lands lay along either side of the old turnpike from Andover bridge northward, with a great pasture on the easterly slope of Tower Hill, the lands of one Alpheus Bodwell, being in the Ward Five lowlands. West of the railway was the modest low dwelling of Captain John Smith, on the site of the residence of E. F. Childs, Esq., at the corner of Haverhill and May streets. One Jennings, formerly owned the lands northward of this dwelling nearly to Methuen line. Two dwellings, not particularly noticeable, stood on the slope of the hill before reaching the Bodwell farm buildings, just westward of the ferry road. This Bodwell farm house has within a year or two been supplanted by a modern brick structure; the estate is still held by the family. Asa M. Bodwell, Esq., being one of the few men of enterprise remaining of the old stock of settlers born and reared upon the soil. Edwin Sargent, Esq., residing on Prospect Hill, is another enterprising native who has faithfully kept the inheritance. Warren Stevens, Esq., of South Lawrence, was to the manor born, and with others worthily represents the old stock in that locality. Of the descendants of James Smith, who had a small estate on the old turnpike just north of Haverhill street, Charles M. Smith is a man whose example may be safely followed and his *walk* commended. The original Poors, Barnards, Liscombs, Gages and Swans have worthy descendants, holding in many cases portions of the old estate.

On the farm of Levi Emery, Esq., our lively Representative, was the old farm house formerly of one Ordway, a sterling Bunker Hill patriot, who, when ammunition failed, threw stones and clods, and possibly hurled imprecations at the red coats. The estate was afterwards owned by one Trull.

The Samuel Ames, formerly Davis, farm was the same substantially as that now owned by Mr. Ames, and below, at the river banks and ferry, were two ancient houses, once much resorted to in the days of ferries and fords. A rickety dwelling known as the Roger house stood at upper guard locks, and was the first to be demolished and replaced at the founding of the city.

On the lower Spicket was the Foster house, still standing, just below East Haverhill street bridge, and the paper mills of A. Durant, Esq., long since supplanted and removed. The little old school house at the corner of East Haverhill and Prospect streets, was long since replaced by a modern spacious building; the one on Tower Hill was years ago removed; the one in South Lawrence was removed years since and is now a modest dwelling.

Where is now the Arlington Mills, stood the piano case factory of Abiel Stevens, afterwards transformed into a hat factory, and in the immediate neighborhood the residence of father and son; the well-known Susan Huse place, the house standing, the residence lately occupied by John N. Archer, and the square house, in which, in the early days, Nathan Wells, Esq., resided.

In South Lawrence the cross-road settlement, where Andover street crosses Broadway, was the nearest approach to a village within the present city limits. Here was the Essex Tavern, the Shawsheen Tavern and county store. The substantial brick residence of the late Hon. Daniel Saunders, is still standing and occupied by his respected widow. The Essex House is now a dwelling, changed somewhat from its former appearance. The Shawsheen House under another name is still kept as a public house. Opposite the old toll house was a modest old style dwelling.

On the Lowell road westward from this corner are three old dwellings of note. The Theodore Poor farm house, the Caleb Richardson

HEZEKIAH PLUMMER,

Lumber Dealer, 434 Haverhill St.; residence, 155 Haverhill St. Born in Andover territory now Lawrence, in 1815. He was brought up on a farm, commencing to learn the carpenter's trade when thirteen years old. Was engaged in making doors and sashes in 1846, at Hazen Mill, formerly so called, on the Lowell road, about a mile from South Lawrence depot, Soon after this, when there commenced a demand for lumber to build the "new city," he erected a steam mill upon the South Side, for the same purpose. Associated with Joseph Norris from 1852 until his death, Mr. Plummer has built many public buildings, as well as private residences. Married in 1846; has one child. Attends the Unitarian church. Was common councilman in 1856 and 1859; alderman, 1861, 1868, 1871 and 1872.

estate and the old dwellings erected by the pioneers Barnard and Stevens, all with marks of extreme old age, but all showing that they were built by thrifty farmers, men of enterprise, with ideas in advance of their time.

On the corner of Andover and Parker streets, where one Towne lived for years, and John Bailey, Esq., now resides, once stood the dwelling of Capt. Michael Parker. The Captain was a blacksmith as well as farmer; his ancestry were buried in the open lot south of the shop, and as he worked at his forge he could look out upon the little enclosure of sleepers. When he sold his farm of a hundred acres, which lay along the Merrimack eastward, the bodies where removed to Andover cemetery. Parker street perpetuates his name.

In the present suburbs of Lawrence, the old estates remain so nearly as they were and the changes are so well known, descriptions would be tedious. Among the most notable land marks is the Tarbox dwelling at the foot of Clover Hill, where Hon. John K. Tarbox was born, and the old dwelling of the Sargents and Swans, to the eastward of Prospect Hill. Along the line of the Merrimack were rude fish wharves, busy localities in the fishing season; there were five of them between the dam and the Industrial school, simple structures of rough stone and logs, each creating an eddy where at some seasons the fish gathered in immense numbers.

Thus upon the fingers of the hand may be counted the dwellings and buildings that stood within the populous portion of the city. In all the district where the great mills have been built and where men congregate for trade stood not a single habitation. Previous to 1845, little change had taken place for more than a century. The silence that brooded over the plain was almost oppressive. The waterfall wasted a countless horse power in its musical flow, the years came and went and brought little of change to the isolated farmer, the hardy river raftsman, or the careless, happy-go-lucky fisherman who got his supply of food so easily at the rapids, and consumed it in such abundant quantity that, if the modern theory that fish specially nourishes the brain were true, he should have been, as he certainly was not, the most intellectual of mortals.

But, though long delayed, change came, change rapid, radical and entire, overshadowing completely the leaven of original population, till only here and there do we find the descendant of a native family, or a landmark untouched by the hand of enterprise.

CHARLES STORER STORROW,

Treasurer and Agent of the Essex Co. Came to Lawrence from Boston at the founding of the city, surveying its site, locating the streets, improvements, reserves, etc.; a civil engineer by profession, he planned and directed those first important works—the great stone dam and the canals. Born at Montreal, P. Q., March 25, 1809, during the temporary residence of his parents there. Was first mayor of Lawrence, 1853. Manager and engineer of the Boston & Lowell Railroad previous to coming to Lawrence. Chief engineer of operations at Hoosac Tunnel for a time. Appointed one of the park commissioners for the city of Boston in 1876. Has resided in Boston for several years attending to the finances of the company at the Boston office, and constantly visiting Lawrence, attending personally to the home management. Married Lydia Cabot, and has several children.

V.

BEGINNING THE ENTERPRISE.—THE ESSEX COMPANY.

---

* Amid all the gorgeous imagery of the Arabian Night Entertainments, that rich, unfailing source of youthful enjoyment and delight, there has probably no one tale so colored the day dream of boyhood or so materially ministered to the idealistic fancy of imaginative youth, as the enchanting story of "Aladdin and the Wonderful Lamp," wherein is recited among the many marvellous feats of the wonderful Genii, the subservient slave of the youthful possessor of the wonderful lamp. The account is almost incredible, even where one is so ready to believe, of the erection from foundation to turret of a most magnificent palace complete, with its entire equipment, with the exception of one single window, in the short space of a single night.

Substituting in the stead of a single night-time, the space of hardly half a short half decade of years, and here on this very spot of earth called home by thousands there has been performed a feat hitherto hardly less incredible, to wit, in this short space of time, by the aid of no supernatural power or mythical agency, a deep and rapid river, arrested in its impetuous course, its mighty and resistless force

* For a portion of this chapter the compiler is indebted to Hon. W. H. P. Wright for facts and formulated sentences.

made the subservient slave of man, and doomed to toil in harness at the will of its master, the erection of an infant city, with its mills and its hundreds of diversified industries, its churches, its schools, its happy homes, and all the manifold surroundings that go to make up a happy, prosperous, flourishing municipality, and all this on a barren locality, which before afforded but a moderate support to a few unambitious tillers of the soil.

DANIEL SAUNDERS, SR.

If the earliest conception of the scheme and the means of its successful acheivements, if the unshared labor and responsibility, the heart-sickening discouragement, the wearing anxiety and care necessarily attendant on so vast an undertaking in its inception, are matters of moment. If to the unfailing sagacity, the untiring energy, and indomitable resolution of one man, the success of an enterprise is mainly due, and all these together in one individual, entitle him to rank as Founder of the Enterprise, then to one who unassuming and unpretending, for many years, walked with us and lived amongst us, belongs the proud title of the Founder of our City, and places among the honored names in Lowell, of Boot, of Colburn and Worthen of earlier days, that of Daniel Saunders, of Lawrence. Sometime previous to 1835 Mr. Saunders, than resident in Andover, and at the time engaged in the woolen manufacture, on his own account, came by chance into the possession of an old plan for a canal from Lowell to tide water in the Merrimack river. He was a man who never mislaid, or wasted, or destroyed anything that could by any possibillity become of future use or value, unpretending but self reliant, who thought more than he talked, and who was one of the very few possessed of that rare faculty of keeping their own secret without taking the world into their confidence upon every matter trivial or otherwise, or who felt necessary to cackle into existence every new idea suggesting itself, as the hen ushers into the world her new laid egg.

From occasional studies of the plan and from the numerous sites for locking, as thereon portrayed, he was persuaded, that there must be a more considerable fall between Lowell and tide water in the Merrimack river than was generally conceived, and this seemed somewhat plausible from the fact that the river between these two points was navigable downward by rafts, and exhibited at no one place any decided fall, but showed the descent of the water, such as it was, by occasional rapids, up which a boat might be pushed without difficulty in ordinary height of water, and consequently was to an ordinary observer, extremely deceptive as to its actual capacity for power. In order to satisfy himself of the fact, with a single assistant, and with no other instruments than a straight edge and spirit level, he determined the fall of the several rapids, between the two points, with an approximate certainty, sufficiently accurate at any rate for his satisfaction, and thereupon at once was prefigured clear and distinct beyond question in his mind, all the capabilities and advantages of this mighty source of power and wealth, hidden under the unassuming form of a few deceptive rapids. The Genii of the Stream had been evoked from beneath the waters and had been compelled to exhibit himself in all the terrible majesty of his awful power, but not as yet was he subject further to mortal incantation.

From that moment with Mr. Saunders it was only a question of time, only awaiting an opportunity, and the *man* to demonstrate and develop it; nor did he hesitate to talk over in the privacy of his family circle, the probabilities of the growth of a great city on the banks of the Merrimack in Methuen and Andover; whether or no his eyes should ever see it was to him then a matter of doubt, but to the vision of his children, if spared, prophesied, with a certainty that silenced cavil, all that the present has effected in the way of material growth and prosperity in the City of Lawrence.

But the mere discovery of this immense water power, hitherto unknown, unrecognized and unimproved, was only one step, and that a very small one towards its full development.

About two miles above the present location, at the head of Peters Falls, so called, a dam could have been constructed at a much less expenditure of money than where the present dam now stands, but at the sacrifice of a few feet of fall, and it was by no means clear then nor for sometime after to the mind of our enterprising discoverer which of the two, under all circumstances, was the more desirable spot for his purpose; but to his mind one thing was clear, definite, determined, and that was that the scheme of founding, in one of the two localities a great manufacturing centre, was far from visionary and that sooner or later, by some person in some way and by some means it would be brought about; consequently, on his own account, without taking any one outside of his own immediate family into his

ALBERT WARREN,

Commission Merchant, 21 Broadway; residence, 274 Haverhill St. Came to Lawrence in April, 1850. Born at Leicester, Mass., Sept., 1814. Is a card clothing manufacturer by trade, and commenced that business in this city under the firm name of Smith, Walker & Co., which changed to Warren & Bryant, and subsequently to Warren & Robinson. Mr. Warren retired six years since. Is married but has no children. Attends the Lawrence Street Congregational church. Was alderman the first year of the city charter, and was mayor in 1855 and 1856.

councils, in 1840 he purchased of Frederick Noyes a strip of land about a third of a mile in length, which took in Peters Falls on the south side of the river.

Nothing more was done in this direction until 1843, when he effected a purchase from Joseph Griffin, of Lowell, of an island covered with wood, situate at the head of Peters Falls, which island is now flooded, and is below the level of the flowing river, out of sight beneath the deep waters. Later in the same year, he bought of Samuel Griffin a strip of land about half a mile in length, containing some eighty acres in the whole, on the north side, and from time to time, as opportunity afforded, quietly effected purchases of several different parties, until he held in his own right the whole of Peters Falls, and had secured to himself the key to the mighty power of the great river, which under his purchases, by means of the flowage laws of Massachusetts, could neither be wrested from him, nor could his right to utilize the same be hindered, although the other land owners on the river should grudgingly refuse to sell whatever might be necessary for the full enjoyment of his privilege so secured for a reasonable compensation ; and so judiciously did he set himself at work, and so quietly was all this effected that no person other than the confidents in his own immediate family circle suspected even the existence of the hidden giant, much less did they imagine it within the range of probabilities that in their day he would be summoned from out the waters to demonstrate before their eyes, in active industrial energy, the capabilities of his terrible presence and matchless power.

Having now proceeded as far as he could well venture singly and alone in an undertaking so vast, and having just at this time disposed of his woolen business, he was now at liberty to give to the enterprise his undivided attention, provided he could enlist in its behalf associated capital, which in no inconsiderable amount would be required in order to carry forward towards its completion the grand project in which he was so heartily enlisted, in which he had such entire faith, to which he had given so much thought and study, and for the full development of which, in its entirety, he was now prepared to devote himself, to the exclusion of all other matters of business whatsoever. He accordingly opened the whole matter to his nephew, J. G. Abbott, John Nesmith and Samuel Lawrence, all then residents of Lowell, disclosing as well what he had done and what he already knew in the premises, as also what in his opinion the future promised and required.

He found the parties readily disposed to give the project their favorable consideration, well knowing that he was a person whose judgment was least likely to be warped by his enthusiasm, and waiting only to satisfy themselves of the actual fall in the Merrimack River below Hunt's Falls in Lowell, in full sympathy with him they entered into his views, and immediately thereupon was formed the Merrimack Water Power Association embracing, together with the first named, Daniel Saunders, Jr., then a law student in Lowell, Thomas Hopkinson and Jonathan Tyler of Lowell, and Nathaniel Stevens of Andover.

Of course it was an object of prime importance to obtain the title to as much of the land as possible adjacent to the location determined upon, as well to secure the advantage of controlling everything relating to the laying out of the future municipality in its early embryo state, as also to reap the advantage of the immediate rise in the value of the real estate in the vicinity of the contemplated improvements. How to do this was one of the first questions that presented itself to the newly formed association.

Prominent members of the association urged the importance of at once purchasing, in as quiet a manner as possible, lands in the immediate vicinity of the projected enterprise at the most advantageous bargains, and to an extent as general as possible.

But to him who had studied the whole matter, even in its minute detail, and who had seemingly provided for almost every conceivable contingency, this appeared not the part of wisdom, and his suggestion on the contrary was, that since the exact location was by no means

JOHN RODMAN ROLLINS,

Accountant at Pacific Mills. Residence, 39 Prospect St. Has been a resident for over twenty years. Born in Newburyport Feb. 9, 1817. Was a graduate of Dartmouth College, of the Class of '36, subsequent to which he taught school 12 years. Married Sarah Stearns Patterson Nov. 20, 1844; has two children. Is a regular attendant at the Lawrence Street Congregational Church. Was for thirteen years paymaster of the Essex Company. Was mayor of Lawrence for the years 1857 and 1858. Captain in the Union Army, 1863-4. Since Dec. 1866 Mr. Rollins has been paymaster at the Pacific Mills.

at the time definitely determined, the superior advantages of the present locality in height of fall being offset by the dimnuition of outlay required to build a dam at Peters Falls, two miles above, and as the purchase of outlands at both places would necessarily secure a loss on one portion or the other, he advised that the association should at once proclaim their purpose and intention of commencing in one of the two localities hereafter to be determined as the interest of the association should be best subserved, the erection of a new manufacturing city, and offering to the land owners about the location fortunate in being selected a joint benefit with the associates in the enterprise by taking from all owning lands in either vicinity bonds for the conveyance of their lands within a certain time at prices much in advance of their value, present or prospective under the present existing state of things.

To the good judgment of the other associates the suggestions of the original projector at once recommended themselves, and he accordingly commenced taking bonds from the land owners in and about both localities. It was a somewhat slow and tedious process. Few had any idea at the commencement that the scheme would ever amount to anything, and they had no particular objection for a nominal consideration to bind themselves to sell within a given time their farms for one-half more perhaps than they had ever dreamed of realizing for them, but parties could not be hurried; many required repeated visits and almost endless conferences. Absent parties required hunting up and communicating with, and the thousand causes for delay attendant upon an undertaking so vast were, of course, not wanting. The scheme was by the wise ones (and there are many such in every country village) facetiously designated as Saunders' folly. Timid proprietors, who had probably never made a conveyance of a foot of land in their lifetime, hesitated, through mere dread of putting name to paper; these had to be encouraged; the stubborn coaxed; the cautious satisfied. It was not a community of business men that were to be dealt with, but a community of yoemen who mostly held the same land which their fathers had occupied before them, and which, through course of descent, had been somewhat widely distributed. Any other than a most resolute and self-reliant man would have been discouraged at the very outset. But, in the course of time, the sagacity of his plan in relation to bonding the land, was apparent.

It was at first intended to secure a bond for a deed, but afterwards it was deemed more desirable to procure a conditional deed to be signed by all parties, thus making a more binding agreement upon all the parties to the contract. The deed was made in warranty form upon receipt of one hundred dollars or such sum as might be agreed upon, *provided* that Mr. Saunders should pay to the grantor within one year, or such time as agreed upon, the sum of $5000, more or less, as called for in the deed. This sum was not to include the bonus, which in case the enterprise fell threw, was a gratuity to the owners of the land. These bonuses were to come from the sum of $50,000, put up by the association to pave the way for the enterprise, or rather to be expended in the experiment. It was first proposed to call the location "Saunders," but to this proposition Mr. Saunders objected, giving as his reason that there was not in Massachusetts a town called Merrimack, and as this was located on a river of that name, it was eminently fitting and proper that the name given should be "Merrimack," and it was so called up to the time of incorporation. When the act of incorporation was asked of the General Court, it was proposed to give it the name of Lawrence, in honor of the Lawrence family, who were foremost in the manufacturing interest (cotton and woolen) in Massachusetts, and accordingly it was duly incorporated as Lawrence. Many no doubt will wonder why Mr. Saunders declined to give the thing virtually of his own creating, his name, as by so doing his name would have been carried down to latest times, but there is no cause for wonder. He was not ambitious of a name and fame on paper, and no doubt he felt, did his enterprise succeed, his monument and memory would be found in the noble factories

DANIEL SAUNDERS,

Attorney-at-Law; office 246 Essex St. Born in Andover, Mass., October 6, 1822. Graduated from the Harvard Law School in 1844; admitted to the bar July 1, 1845, and has since continued a leading member of the same in Essex County. He was actively engaged with his father, the late Daniel Saunders, in purchasing lands and assisting him in his original enterprise of founding the present city of Lawrence. In 1843 there was formed the Merrimack Water Power Association, having for its object the development of the present water power of Lawrence. Of this association Mr. Saunders was a member. From this association grew the Essex Company which was chartered in 1845, of which since its inception he has been a stockholder, and for many years one of its directors. He has been a member of both branches of the Legislature; was Mayor of the city in 1860, the year of the memorable Pemberton disaster; is married and has four children, and is a member of Grace Episcopal church.

that should line the banks of the noble river in the new city yet in embryo.

As soon as all preliminary arrangements were made, Mr. Saunders immediately devoted his entire services to securing all the necessary land under the conditional deeds we have mentioned, and his success was gratifying, when the many difficulties with which he was forced to contend are taken into consideration, and in eighteen months, he had succeeded in securing all the land upon each side of the river, included in what is now the city of Lawrence, with the following exceptions: On the south side of the river was a lot in the possession of Mr. Samuel Poor, of about thirty acres, which was heavily mortgaged to Mr. N. W. Hazen of Andover, in whose possession it afterwards fell. This lot, upon which stands the Webster House, he was unable to secure, as also a lot of twelve acres on the North Andover road, owned by Mr. Foster, and an undivided fourth of one acre at the south end of the Andover Bridge, upon which stands Gage's Block, now occupied by Emerson Woods as a hotel. These were the only lots upon the South Side remaining in the hands of the original possessors. On the north side of the Merrimack was a lot owned by Fairfield White of six acres, east of Amesbury and south of Haverhill streets. The house of Moses Perkins, Esq., stands nearly upon the southeast corner of this lot. At this time Mr. White was working upon the Boston and Lowell railroad, and offered the land and the buildings upon it for $600. Mr Saunders offered to give a bonus of $200, and agree to take the lot at $1200, if the association should find it advisable to go on with the enterprise. Mr. White at once refused to take less than $1200, but would sell at that price, which offer Mr. Saunders refused to consider, and meeting Messrs. Lawrence and Nesmith and laying the matter before them, was at once advised by Mr. Lawrence to pay the amount demanded. Mr. Saunders differed from this proposition, stating that in his opinion it would be a very unwise proceeding, inasmuch as that should it be known that Mr. White had been paid in hand double his price, the next owner approached would demand perhaps $20,000 for his territory, and the next one perhaps $100,000, and thus no more land could be bought, and the enterprise must per force end there, but that in his opinion it would be more advisable to leave Mr. White in possession, as it would be cheaper in the end to pay him $12,000 than $1200 at that stage. This sound advice was accepted, and in the end Mr. White retained one acre, selling the balance, five acres, to the association for $12,000. The only other exception on the north side was about one-half acre on Broadway, then Turnpike, owned by Mr. Smith, and still in possession of his widow and heirs. Thus it will be seen with how much energy and fidelity Mr. Saunders prosecuted his duty as the land agent of the association, in this, the most delicate and arduous duty connected with the enterprise, and if he was doubly successful in securing this property and at the same time securing a competence for himself, no one should envy or begrudge the success rightfully earned, and to which no shade of chicanery or fraud can attach.

No one can say that his or her property was not bought for far above true value, and when it is taken into consideration that many of the farms were heavily mortgaged, and must soon have fallen into the hands of the creditors, we see that the debtor, instead of being turned out of doors with neither house or farm, received a sum more than sufficient to free him from debt, and still leave him with more property than was in his possesion when the millstone of debt was contracted. Many, no doubt regret to this day that they disposed of their property, but it should be borne in mind that without this disposition, they and their children would still possess a few barren and unproductive acres,—and nothing more. The total amount of land thus secured by Mr. Saunders, including lands in Andover and the flowage to Lowell, amounted to between three and four thousand acres.

The price which the land owners were to receive in case the projected enterprise was a success, induced many to give bonds at once,

WILLIAM H. P. WRIGHT,

Retired Lawyer. Residence, 55 East Haverhill St. Born at Lowell in 1827. Educated at Cambridge University. Studied law with his father in Lowell, coming to this city in 1847, and continuing study with Daniel Saunders, and also with Wright & Flanders. Commenced practice with his brother Thomas, which partnership continued till 1861, or about the time he was elected mayor, which position he held in 1862-63, two of the most important years of our city's history. Subsequent to this Mr. Wright practiced law until 1876. He represented the city in the legislature in 1867-68, and officiated as judge during the interim between Judge Stevens and Judge Harmon. Has a wife and one son.

and as a general thing these were parties who were most conversant with business affairs, whose judgment was generally to be relied upon, and who exerted in the community a certain influence on that account, and they soon became active interested agents in inducing others to do the same; and as it was understood that the ultimate location depended largely upon the unanimity of feeling among the land holders of either locality over the others, in bonding their real estate, there grew up a rivalry between the land owners of the different places to secure each for themselves the advantage dependent on each ultimate location by enlisting as universally as possible every party in interest into the general movement, yet in a country as sparsely populated as this then was, rapid interchange of news was out of the question. Everything moved, but it moved slow, and the most untiring energy and unflagging zeal was constantly required to keep even that movement continuous. Many months of hard, discouraging, continuous labor ensued before the title to the real estate was in this way generally secured. When taken into consideration the fact that in a city two miles square, almost the entire real estate through the efficacy of these bonds came into the hands of the parties in interest, and that two miles further up river a like condition of things existed had the location there been fixed, when you bear in mind that all this was the result of the labors of one man, for in this delicate duty subordinates could not well be employed or trusted, you can form some idea of the patience and policy requisite, the visitations and journeyings necessary, the arguments and inducements required, the objections and scruples silenced, the doubts removed, the questions answered, the enquiries satisfied and the caution and judgment exercised before any such result could have been brought about. Few are the men who would have undertaken such a task, and fewer yet those who could so satisfactorily have accomplished it. The patience under difficulties, the resolution of purpose, the rugged common sense, the intimate knowledge of mankind that were marked characteristics of Mr. Saunders, visibly manifest themselves in this achievement.

After seventy-six years of tireless activity, in which few days could be counted as lost, and none as wasted, on the eighth day of October, 1872, he gave o'er his labors, laid aside his cares, disrobed himself of his infirmities and found

"Rest at last,
Repose complete, eternal,
Love, rest and home."

Near the summit of one of the lofty hills that overlooks the city at whose birth he was so conspicuous in action, he was by loving hands tenderly laid away, where "he rests from his labors, and his works do follow him."

On the twentieth day of March, 1845, the legislature of Massachusetts granted to Samuel Lawrence, John Nesmith, Daniel Saunders and Edmund Bartlett their associates and successors, the charter of the Essex Company, authorizing among other things the construction of a dam across the Merrimack River, either at Deer Jump Falls or Bodwell's Falls, or at some point in the river between the two falls. From this time Daniel Saunders, although still employed in busily adjusting matters of detail in relation to the various conveyances of real estate, the adjustment of damages for flowage, and matters of that nature for and on account of the Essex Company, steps aside as the principal character upon the theatre of action.

On the sixteenth of the following April, the stock ($1,000,000) having in the meantime been taken up, the company was organized with Abbott Lawrence, Nathan Appleton, Ingnatus Sargent, William Sturgis and Charles Storrow as directors. Mr. Storrow was elected agent and chief engineer. At the present time he is treasurer of the company. Mr. Storrow at once began work with a corps of assistants, and an accurate survey was made, plans executed for a dam, canal, mill sites, streets, lots and public squares in the town, and on the first day of

ALFRED J. FRENCH,

Homœopathic Physician. Residence and place of business, 44 Lawrence Street. Has been in Lawrence twenty-one years; practiced in Methuen seven years. Was born in Bedford, N. H. in 1823, and received an academic education at Hancock (N. H.) Literary Seminary. Labored on a farm until the age of twenty. Received a medical education at the Vermont Medical College, graduating in 1848. Was married in 1852 to Sarah A. Hardy of Antrim, N. H.; has no children living, having buried an only daughter. Dr. French is a member of the First Baptist church, chairman of its finance committee, and was treasurer for five years. Served as overseer of the poor in 1858; representative to legislature in 1859-60; elected mayor for 1864; served as president of Lawrence National Bank five years from its organization, and is a trustee of the Broadway Savings Bank.

August work was begun, and the first stone laid in the company's dam September 19, and in a little over two years the work was complĕted. The dam is one of the most remarkable structures in the country. It is of granite, 1,629 feet in length, thirty-five feet thick at the base and 12 1-2 at the top, backed by gravel to within a few feet of the surface. It is bedded into the bed-rock of the river. The granite blocks from which the dam is built were hammered on the bed and laid in hydraulic cement. The dam cost $250,000. The overflow of water is 900 feet wide, and the fall is twenty-six feet. The dam is in some places as high as forty and one-third feet.

The charter provided that the dam should be so built as not to flow Hunt's Falls at Lowell, and made provision for a commission of three competent persons to fix and by permanent monuments determine the point in the river which is the foot of Hunt's Falls.

After the completion of the dam it was found that owing to the friction and consequent obstruction of water by the turns in the river, which was not taken in account, the water flowed back upon Hunt's Falls further than the fixed monument, and consequently some sixteen inches were hammered off from the top of the great stone headers which project over the fall of the dam, thus seriously interferring with the perfect symmetry of the structure, and much impairing its beauty. The charter further required that a suitable and reasonable fishway should be built and maintained in the dam, to be kept open at such seasons as are necessary and usual for the passage of fish, and provided that the county commissioners of Essex county upon application should prescribe the mode of constructing the same. Accordingly a place was prepared by the Essex Company, which the county commissioners accepted and prescribed as a proper form of fishway to be built. The county commissioners were evidently not first-class fresh water fishermen, however reliable might have been their judgment in the matter of deep sea fishing. They were probably strongly influenced by a perverted agricultural taste, for their fishway was a modified swill trough of immense strength, extending diagonally from the top of the dam to the river bed on the southerly side, and across this trough at equal distances, were spiked great cross timbers, against which the water was to strike, and thus form eddies, and over these timbers the fish were to leap in sportive glee. On the original plan the happy fish was pictured out, wiggling in the imaginary eddies, hopping merrily over the cross timbers, speeding rapidly through or resting in confiding innocence in the cool waters of a seductive eddy, their tails fairly squirming with delight, and their countenances beaming with astonished wonderment at the skill displayed, as well as the unmistakable gratitude for kindness exhibited, on the part of their old destroyer and arch-enemy, man. The picture was a pleasing one; future generations may prize it, but as an avenue for the migration of fish the project was a failure. Since that time various devices have been constructed to serve the important purpose, but none seemed to meet the requirements until the summer of 1876, when under the direction of the State fish commissioners a way was constructed which in part seems to be satisfactory. To induce the finny tribe to poke their noses in that direction a large sum was expended in blasting from the foot of the way to deep water near the dam. It is now thought that through the labor which has been bestowed on the artificial breeding of salmon the river will be re-stocked at no very distant day.

The north canal is a little over a mile long, 100 feet wide at the upper, and sixty feet wide at the lower end, and twelve feet deep. It is 400 feet distant from the river and parallel with it. The engineer in charge of the construction of the dam was Charles A. Bigelow, a captain of engineers in the United States army, and under his supervision the dam and north canal were completed in 1848. The river affords on an average about 5000 cubic feet of water a second, but sometimes it reaches 60,000. A power thus obtained is estimated at 150 mill power. A mill power is calculated to take thirty cubic feet of water a second, with a head and fall of twenty-five feet. This gives a

NATHANIEL P. H. MELVIN,

Hardware Dealer at 582 Essex St. Residence on Bodwell St. Has been in Lawrence twenty-five years. Born in Lowell in 1825. For twenty years after coming to this city he was chief engineer at the Washington Mills, resigning that most important position to embark in the hardware trade. Mr. Melvin is the only man who has had the honor of being elected to the mayoralty chair of Lawrence for three terms, he having occupied that position in 1867, 1868 and 1870. He was also alderman in 1860. At present he is a member of the Lawrence Water Board. Attends the Episcopal church.

force estimated to equal from 60 to 70 horse power. When the Atlantic Mills Corporation bought their mill site the price agreed upon for a mill power was $14,333 of which $9,333 was paid in cash, the balance of $5,000 remaining perpetually at 4 per cent. interest, payable annually in silver or its equivalent. The Atlantic Company bought twenty mill powers, and the other corporations more or less as to their requirements.

The Essex Company has continued to sell mill powers to manufacturers upon such terms as deemed prudent between the parties. After the sales had been made to the larger corporations they advanced somewhat in the price for several years, though the last sale, which was on the South Canal, to N. W. Farwell & Son for bleachery, netted the company only $12,000. "Each mill power is declared to be the right to draw from the nearest canal or water course of the grantors so much water as shall give a power equal to thirty cubic feet of water per second, when the head and fall is twenty-five feet; and no more is to be drawn in any one second, nor is the same to be drawn more than sixteen hours in each day of twenty-four hours; and in order to prevent disputes as to the power of each mill privilege in the variations of the height of water from changes of the season or other causes, it is understood and declared that the quantity of water shall be varied in proportion to the variation of the height, one foot being allowed and deducted from the height of the actual head and fall, and also from that with which it is compared before computing the proportion between them: thus on a head and fall of thirty feet the quantity of water to be used would be twenty-four cubic feet, and 24-100 of a cubic foot per second."

A second canal, on the south side of the river, was commenced in 1870; the upper section is completed, the mill sites sold, and substantial brick buildings already erected thereon; this canal is to be extended as fast as the power is in demand, to be finally about one and one-fourth miles in length, emptying into Shawsheen River. The capital stock of the company was reduced some years ago to $800,000 by cancellation of stock received for land, and again in 1872, by the payment to stockholders of $30.00 per share surplus funds, was reduced to $500.000.

On the 28th of April, 1846, when there were but few other than temporary houses, the Essex Company, having completed their plans of the streets and lots of the new town, advertised the public sale of land; large numbers flocked to the place, and amid the open fields, the fields marked off by the furrow of a plow, before the barren waste of sand stretching down to the river where now stand the Pacific and Washington Mills, the red flag of the auctioneer marked the sale by the foot of lots from the farms so recently purchased at a low price by the acre. The prices obtained were deemed fabulous, and by many ruinous, but faith in the future of the new city and the ability of its founders was not misplaced, and although the business revulsions of latter years have depressed some of the property, there is not a foot of it sold at that time but would to-day pay a fair and most of it a very handsome profit upon the investment. The highest price then obtained was for the lot upon the corner of Essex and Jackson streets, opposite Clarke's apothecary store, which realized seventy cents per square foot; other lots on Essex street were sold at prices from fifty-eight to thirty cents; lots on Haverhill street were sold at from nine to thirteen cents per foot.

On the 6th day of December, 1855, the Essex Company offered at public auction about 600 house lots in various parts of the city. Some of these purchasers who retained their land for a series of years realized well upon their investments; but many other lots somewhat remote from the centre of business, have never had a market value sufficient to pay the original purchase with interest. The hard times of 1857 soon came on, and it almost seemed by the numerous lots placarded "for sale" that every real estate holder in the city desired to dispose of his property. But these gradually wore away, till nearly

SMITH BROWNING WILKINSON DAVIS,

Merchant Tailor; has been in business on Essex Street from 1854 to 1878; residence, 20 Park St. Has been in Lawrence nearly twenty-five years. Was born at Foster, R. I., Apr. 13th, 1824. Learned his trade in Scituate, R. I. Was educated at Lapham Institute, R. I. His boyhood was spent on a farm. Married Lorinda Bishop in 1848; has two children. Is connected with the Free Baptist church. Mr. Davis was a member of the common council for 1869-70, officiating as president during the latter year; was mayor for 1871-2, and is at present clerk of the overseers of the poor.

all the available lots have been utilized and become the homes of prosperous thousands.

During 1848, the Essex Company proffered the city a tract comprising 17 2-3 acres, which they had wisely reserved, to be kept as a public common, the city to expend not less than $300 per year for twenty years in its adornment. After some misgivings on the part of the citizens the offer was accepted and to-day the city can boast one the finest parks in New England, outside of Boston. The Essex Company has since given three other parcels of land to the city for the purposes of public parks, with certain restrictions, which have been accepted. These are Storrow Park, Prospect Hill, one in Ward V and the other in Ward VI, which have been fenced, but little has been done towards beautifying them. The company has also given to several of the religious denominations sites for church edifices.

The Essex Company still retains the control of the dam and water power of the river, which is now believed to be equivalent to 10,000 horse power, 7,200 of which have been sold and utilized. The remainder is ready for sale or lease. The company still owns many house lots and other tracts of real estate, and employs on the average about twenty-five men to care for their interests. The officers of the company are: Charles S. Storrow, Treasurer, Boston; H. F. Mills, Engineer, Lawrence; Robert H. Tewksbury, Cashier, Lawrence.

VI.

ANDOVER BRIDGE.—THE OLDEST CORPORATION.

---

* Commencing before the present century, the records of the proprietors of Andover bridge, still carefully preserved, contain the history of that oldest and only very old work of a corporation within Lawrence limits.

In the year 1793, in the closing years of the first administration of George Washington, when, released from the burdens imposed by the Revolution, men of enterprise engaged once more in peaceful callings and projected home improvements, an Act was passed by the General Court of Massachusetts incorporating Samuel Abbott and John White, Esquires, with Joseph Stephens, merchant, and Ebenezer Poor, yoeman, and associates, as a body politic, under the name of the "Proprietors of Andover Bridge," for the purpose of erecting a bridge over Merrimack River from Andover to Methuen, at Bodwell's Falls, where our Broadway bridge now stands. March 19, 1793, John Hancock, then governor, affixed his bold signature approving the act. This charter provided that the bridge should be built within three years, should not be less than twenty-eight feet wide, should have a

* Hon. R. H. Tewksbury.

JOHN KEMBLE TARBOX,

Attorney and Counsellor-at-Law. Office, Essex Savings Bank Building, Essex Street; residence, 17 Valley Street. Mr. Tarbox was born in that part of Methuen now embraced within the limits of Lawrence, May 6, 1838. He studied the profession of law in the office of Col. Benjamin F. Watson, and was admitted to the bar in 1860. While a student-at-law he edited the *Lawrence Sentinel* newspaper. Served in the Union Army in the Fourth Regiment Massachusetts Volunteers. Was a delegate to the Democratic National Convention at Chicago, in 1864, and an alternate delegate at large from the State to the Democratic National Convention in 1868, and candidate for Presidential Elector. He was representative to the General Court in 1868, 1870 and 1871, and State Senator in 1872. Mayor of Lawrence in 1873 and 1874, and a member of the 44th Congress from the Seventh Massachusetts District.

centre span of one hundred ten feet reach, over the main channel, to insure easy passage for great timber rafts.

Tolls were fixed by the act for foot passengers and every kind of carriage from a chariot to a wheelbarrow. By two additional acts the proprietors were allowed to increase tolls. By the first act they were given the right to charge tolls for fifty years, by an additional act this right was extended to seventy-five years; by a second additional act they were given monopoly forever with right to reduce the width of the bridge, when rebuilt, from twenty-eight to twenty feet. Subscribers to stock formally organized the company immediately after incorporation. The directors without delay set about the work of building, a master mechanic was hired, timber was purchased, and the work went bravely on.

The first structure stood on huge wooden piers, and cost 3,998 pounds 13 shillings and nine pence, as the account is made up, or in modern round numbers, twelve thousand dollars.

The opening of the bridge, Tuesday, November 19th, 1793, was a great local event. The ministers of Methuen and Andover, with stockholders, and principal men of Essex, and Rockingham, were invited, the directors, voting to "entertain" on that day.

Captain Dunkin's company of infantry and Stephen Barker's company of cavalry appear to have done escort duty. A boy named Stevens, undertaking to pass the guard stationed to keep the bridge clear for invited dignitaries was bayoneted by a soldier named Foster, and died from the effect of his injuries in a few days. Bridge building experience was limited then, and the new structure had an ailing existence of only eight or nine years. August 28th, 1801, a part of the bridge fell in ruins while a drove of cattle were passing over it. Of the herd 59 sheep, 6 cows and a horse, saddled and bridled, perished in the waters below, and were paid for by the afflicted proprietors.

In the winter of 1802-3, the superstructure of the bridge was rebuilt, upon the piers of the old, by Asa Town, Esq., contractor. It was a truss bridge of three frame arches and one—the great centre arch—of solid boards or plank. This form of arch, now very common, proved defective, and the great centre span fell in ruins causing delay, expense and discouragement. It was promptly repaired, but only four years thereafter, February 15th, 1807, a great freshet and run of ice swept away the larger part of the bridge. Then the proprietors petitioned the General Court for leave to raise money by lottery to rebuild, but they were refused the privilege.

Previous to this re-building, the bridge had stood on the site of the present railroad bridge; this new structure was moved up stream to the present location, and permanent stone piers were substituted for wood. These piers, at times terribly damaged by ice and logs, and since increased in height and thoroughly repaired, now support the present structure, excepting that the northern and southern abutments have been entirely rebuilt, the former somewhat inland to clear the plunge of the dam. The first northern pier was reconstructed after the great freshet and jam of logs in 1870.

In 1837 the late John Wilson, of Methuen, built the old structure upon which many of the first comers to the new city rode over more than thirty years ago. It was a primitive sort of affair without sidewalks, the entire width of twenty feet was still further reduced by huge strengthening timbers within the high board railing, leaving but seventeen feet of passage way crowded with travelers flocking in and teams loaded with material for the dam, canal, new buildings and mill foundations from the ledges of South Lawrence and elsewhere.

The latter history of the bridge is well known. The Essex Company absorbed it in 1846. In the spring of 1848, the structure was rebuilt and raised nearly ten feet to the level of the railway line by Stone & Harris, contractors. The new structure was a frame truss of the Howe patent. Stephen P. Simmons, Esq., a present resident,

ROBERT HASKELL TEWKSBURY,

Cashier of the Essex Company. Born in Hopkinton, N. H., April 11, 1833. Has been in Lawrence twenty-seven years. Was a member of the Board of Assessors in 1862–3. City Treasurer and Collector from 1864 to 1874. Mayor of Lawrence 1875. A member of the board having in charge the Lawrence Water Works since the completion of the same. Is secretary of the Old Residents' Association or Local Historical Society of Lawrence. Married Angelia C. Hawthorne, November, 1859; has two sons living. Resides at 249 Jackson St.

raised and thoroughly repaired the piers at this time. In the great freshet of 1852, the toll-house, south abutment and fishway all went down in the rush of waters.

In 1858 the bridge was thoroughly and economically reconstructed by Morris Knowles, Esq., who is still active in life's duty, on the present plan of arches supporting from beneath.

An Act of the legislature of 1868, secured mainly by efforts of our townsman, the Hon. John K. Tarbox, resulted in the laying out of this and Lawrence bridge below as a public highway. There was much rejoicing at this newly acquired freedom from tolls which had been imposed for three quarters of a century, although by the county commissioners' award the city was saddled with the expense of maintaining it forever. Judge N. W. Harmon, served for many years as clerk and treasurer of this corporation, and Hon. John R. Rollins succeeded him.

June 20th, 1825, a large number of citizens from the region round about, congregated upon the old bridge to welcome General Lafayette in his triumphal journey from Boston to Concord, N. H., and the north. He traveled in an open carriage, with richly caparisoned horses, and was attended by noted men. Andover cavalry and several companies of infantry acted as escort. At Methuen he met and recognized an old infantry soldier of his corps, and the citizens marshaled by Major Benjamin Osgood gave him a hearty welcome. The Andover cavalry escorted him to the New Hampshire State line where he was received with honors.

Asa Pettingill, the first toll gatherer, had a salary of ten pounds, $33.33 per year and the use of toll-house and garden. After thirty years the salary was raised, the directors formally voting to allow nine dollars and one gallon of lamp oil per month as salary, and to grant the use of the proprietors' cooking-stove for three dollars rental per annum.

At one time the directors voted to allow all going from Andover to Methuen to church on Sunday to pass free of toll. The toll-man was surprised at the religious interest attracting Andover people to the north bank, but on inquiry could learn of no special awakening. Feeling that their liberality had been abused, they voted to allow only those known to the toll man as church goers to pass free, this involved that official in dispute as to the religious habits of travelers, and it was voted to charge saints and sinners alike, both Sundays and week days. The record shows, however, that the directors voted for several years to allow Adolphus Durant, Esq., with his family to go from Methuen to Andover to church free of toll. They also by repeated votes gave that exemplary and indefatigable pioneer preacher, whose memory is honored and revered, Dr. George Packard, free use of the bridge in his journeys to and from the new parish. This record is valuable, showing that the oldest corporation had a soul, and while everything else paid toll the "good news" went free to the deserving.

Junketing is not a modern custom. The proprietors of our old bridge found solace at the Shawsheen corner taverns where their meetings were held. In the season of 1802, Benjamin Ames, innkeeper at the old Essex House, charged 21 suppers, 19 pints of gin, 4 1-2 mugs of toddy and 4 "boals of punch," with a liberal supply of brandy. The corporation paid 8 pounds, 14 shillings and one penny for these sustaining supplies. Another season they contracted a bill of $13.75 for "rum, brandy, sugar and horse baiting," and the poor horses got but 15 cents worth of supplies. One abstemious and economical director contracted at every meeting the uniform charge of "half a glass of rum and one biscuit." The great bill of liquors came when, in the summer of 1802, they rebuilt the bridge. John and Henry Poor, innkeepers at the Shawsheen, supplied the workmen with one hundred and eleven gallons of N. E. and W. I. rum, and with 142 lbs. of sugar for sweetning; the charge was made

EDMUND R. HAYDEN,

Coal and Wood Dealer at corner of Merrimack St. and Broadway, and Common St., near north depot; residence 81 Tremont St. Resident in Lawrence since 1853. Born at Harvard, Mass., Dec. 23d, 1819. Received an ordinary common school education. Worked at stone cutting until 1851, when he went to California, returning in April, 1853. Married Charlotte Fairbanks, Apr. 4, 1844; has one son. Attends the universalist church. Served as policeman from 1854 until 1863; was marshal at time of Pemberton Mills disaster, 1860. Entered the wood business in 1863 near the depot, where W. P. Clark's store now stands. Bought out Wm. D. Joplin in 1866, and united with F. L. Runals in the wood and coal business, under the firm name of Runals & Hayden. Bought out Mr. Runals in 1874, since conducting business alone. Was chosen mayor in 1875, and held the office in 1876.

in many items, and $142.00 paid out of the company's treasury therefor. No toddy or punch was supplied to laborers, they took rum straight or went dry. Laborers and mechanics then had 67 cents to $1.00 per day; a yoke of oxen could be hired for 84 cents per day. A night's lodging at the old Shawsheen tavern appears, from old bills, to have cost the traveler eight cents; a generous dinner, twenty-five cents; a week's board, one dollar and eighty-four cents.

There was trouble about the toll-man selling rum in the early days. A substantial citizen filed his remonstrance, stating that he sold the land on which the toll-house stands with the understanding that grog should never be sold thereon, but he states that said toll-house is known to be a flourishing grog-shop. In reading this protest one admires this old pioneer temperance reformer for a moment, but loses faith in him when he plainly states further on, that by reason of such sale his own business as a seller of grog at the corner, half a mile beyond, had been ruined, and he has been compelled to close his house of entertainment. The proprietors appointed a committee to secure a toll-man who would not sell grog. No doubt they were successful as Deacon James D. Herrick, sat at the receipt of tolls twenty-two years, faithfully bearing witness against rum and rum-selling as the vilest of abominations, the most flagrant of evils.

What a sight it would be to stand upon this old thoroughfare as it was four score years ago, and see the old-time preachers of Andover and Methuen ambling over the shaking timbers, clad in saintly garb, the three cornered hat, cleanly broadcloth and clerical wig, mounted upon beasts of subdued aspect, probably a fair orthodox wife on the pillion behind her exemplary lord. The old doctor, with saddle-bags, the one filled with calomel, seneca, salts, emetics and like mild compounds for ordinary cases, the other with lancets, pewter syringes of all sizes, surgeon's cutlery and tooth pulling instruments, sweep by on his mission of healing. The girl of that period, unused to pull-backs and fashions' devices, sat in the side-saddle as easily and gracefully as the modern belle in the cushioned carriage and cantered over the bridge as lovely and loveable as a womanly woman is in all ages and lands.

On muster and training days the old militia marched over the swaying arches, here and there in the ranks, revolutionary patriots in regimentals, that would now excite derision, but which invested them with more than royal dignity, and awakened all the pride and animation of their patriotic natures. On public days, soldier and citizen drank punch from tubs made of rum-barrels sawn in half. One old resident says he worked all day, when a boy, pounding lemons in these tubs with a maul, earning one cent each tub, and there were six other boys at the same novel employment, in the grounds of the Shawsheen and Essex House, that muster day.

Among the names of stockholders is that of Sir Grenville Temple, of England. Phillips Academy, of Andover, carried a heavy amount for a long time. Much stock was sold for a song for non-payment of assessments.

The half mile from the bridge to the Shawsheen House corner, was the race track in old times, where owners of fast horses tried the speed and endurance of their nags on muster, election and ordination days.

About 1814, some fifteen British officers, prisoners, were quartered under guard at this corner to keep them away from the shipping of the ports. An old lady resident remembers them as excellent dancers, very good looking, very civil and very gallant young men. She added that they were strangely hated by the men, especially the young men, and hate was no name for the feeling of the boys towards the precocious, swaggering little nigger they had for a servant. He tormented the bashful country boys with boasting how his masters would yet conquer the country, banish all the men, marry the prettiest girls and make him overseer of the plantation of Shawsheen Fields.

CALEB SAUNDERS,

Lawyer. Office, Saunders Block, 246 Essex St., residence 6 Andover St. Born in North Andover, Sept. 4th, 1838, and came to Lawrence when five years old. Is the son of Daniel Saunders, Sr., the pioneer of the city. He has resided in Lawrence from its earliest inception. Mr. Saunders received his early education in the common schools, and fitted for college in the high schools; graduated at Bowdoin College in 1859. Married Carrie F. Stickney in 1865; has two children. Is a regular attendant at Grace Episcopal Church. Enlisted in Co. I, 6th Regiment, Apr. 15, 1861, and was with the regiment in its famous march through Baltimore; commissioned first lieutenant in 1st Mass. H. A. in 1862. Member of common council in 1867-9. Alderman in 1873, and mayor in 1877.

The officers and directors of the old company were men of note and ability. Col. Loami Baldwin, first president, was noted civil engineer in his day; of his successors, Major Benjamin Osgood, of Methuen, was a flourishing farmer and householder; Gayton P. Osgood was a member of Congress; Abbott Lawrence was Minister to the Court of St. James; without his word and name Lawrence would not have been founded, his word and gift established the Franklin Library, without which the city might still lack a Public Library. Another, Hon. Charles S. Storrow, engineered and directed the building of the city, and his works praise him in this valley.

The active management of the corporation naturally fell into the hands of Andover and Methuen owners. The first meeting of organization was at the inn of Brinsley Stevens. Mr. Nehemiah Abbott, Captain Caleb Swan, and Mr. Benjamin Poor, were the first resident directors. Mr. Abbott was vice-president of the board, and seems to have been a sort of managing director. Major Joseph Stevens was first treasurer, serving many years; his successors were Captain John Kneeland, Amos Blanchard, Joseph Rice, some of them serving more than twenty years. The first clerk was Deacon John Huse, of Methuen, succeeded by Samuel Abbott Kneeland, Amos Blanchard, Samuel Phillips, John Flint and Joseph Rice.

Hon. John Phillips and Ezra Abbott of Andover, and Zadock Bodwell, of Methuen, were also prominent directors, the former for a time president.

It would amuse modern referees to read the record ordering the employment of a commission of three "artists" to examine the condition of the bridge, and report thereon, and finding the three artists charging collectively *three dollars* for the service. At another time a mechanical "expert" was employed to pass judgment at an expense of a *dollar and a half*. The modern expert and artist would hardly look at the ordinary mortal for those trivial amounts.

An old gentleman tells a story of one of the directors. He was a great farmer, given to experimenting. A spring freshet brought up great quantities of eels, and, subsiding, left them high and dry in pools and hollows. He conceived the idea of boiling them and feeding to swine, of which he had many. His old hired man remonstrated, telling him it was "agin natur to try and fatten pork with fish," besides, Deacon, he says, "if you succeed we shan't know what we're eatin', pork or lamper eels." But the deacon had a cart load of eels drawn up to the barn, he filled the great kettles in the back kitchen with eels, Indian meal and water, kindled the fire and lay down for a doze. But animals that squirm in the frying pan would not submit to boiling without protest, the hot water revived them all and each one became an agonizing serpent. They covered the floor of the old room, writhing in their agony, and knocking the fire brands about the floor. The deacon nerved himself for the contest and commenced the slaughter of the innocents; an old negro, a new comer, who lived with a neighbor, and knew nothing of live eels, heard the outcry, and looking in saw the sea of serpents and fire brands, with the good man laying about him. He ran howling home, saying that more than a thousand devils had got the deacon penned up in the kitchen, but he was fighting and prevailing against them calling mightily on the Lord for help. The deacon said, though they were not Satanic foes, it was the hardest job of his life to subdue those eels, maintain his standing as deacon, and at the same time express himself in language sufficiently emphatic.

Eighty-five years have passed since John Hancock first legalized the charter for the ancient bridge. For half a century thereafter the bridge itself was the solitary evidence of substantial progress in this valley. In all the plain no church spire pointed to heaven, no unusual enterprise disturbed the dreamy quiet; the Merrimack rolled unchecked to the sea. Many a time did our Lawrence pioneer, Daniel Saunders, now gone to his rest, rein up old "Snow Ball," the

JAMES RAE SIMPSON,

Grocer, 343 Essex St.; residence, 24 Lowell St. Has been in Lawrence nearly 26 years. Born at Stanstead, P. Q., Jan. 14, 1832. His Honor James R. Simpson commenced life in humble circumstances. Worked on a farm and attended common school and the Wesleyan Academy, being employed as a teacher when fifteen. Married Julia H. Coan in 1860; has two children. Holds liberal views and attends the Unitarian church. Came to this State in 1849; was first employed in Boston, and afterwards at Manchester, N. H. Print Works, for some time having charge of a room. Removed to Lawrence, intending to pursue the same business, but subsequently entered into mercantile pursuits, in which he is now engaged under firm name of James R. Simpson & Co. Common council, 1863; elected mayor for 1878.

white horse he rode, to the tumbling rapids, as he crossed the old bridge, and dream of the possibility of harnessing that wasting power to the machinery of workshops and mills, thus consummating, as Whittier has it, the marriage of Beauty with Use.

In March, 1845, fourteen gentlemen of means, skill and enterprise, stood upon the bridge, with a newly granted charter to improve the power at these falls. Then and there they rudely conceived the plan which, developed and persistently followed, has dotted this plain with spires, and reared upon the river bank a file of great workshops, the centre and support of ten thousand homes.

The four square miles of barren plain surrounding old Andover bridge are no longer unimportant. Industries have developed thereon, gathering raw material from the wide world and scattering finished products far and near. Old residents by firesides on every hillside and valley of the land, follow with loving interest the fortunes of children who have left their homes, bringing to this new born city strength of muscle, skill of hand, and cunning of brain, to barter as merchandise for honest livelihood and ultimate riches in this labor market of the world's busiest valley.

In humble homes of many lands across the sea old residents doze and dream vaguely of a new and vigorous city on the banks of an American river, where their children thrive by labor and their daughters' children enjoy the new found privileges of free American life.

The prophecy and promise of the old time has been fulfilled. A little one has become a thousand, a small one a strong nation. The solitary place is glad for them; the desert rejoices and blossoms as the rose.

VII.

THE CHURCHES.

It is an incontrovertible fact that the Church of God stands nearer the sympathies of the people than any other institution. So long as men are mortal, religion comes in as a practical solace and support. Human philosophy is no consolation in bereavement. And, though men are learning more every day that true religion should be shrouded in no mystery, the heart can never be made believe that "Marseillaise" and "Yankee Doodle" are as suitable for obsequies as the funeral psalm which hushed the old Christian mother to her last sleep; neither can the lectures of scientists on bioplasms or homogeneous matter fill a void in the human heart.

An All-wise Providence has put it into the hearts of all His rational creatures to worship. It is as natural as it is to love. Every man has his object of adoration and even

> **"The heathen in his blindness**
> **Bows down to wood and stone."**

It is not strange then that the comers to the "new city" should at once cast about them for a place to hold meetings. The men who first came to found the city were of the primitive New England stock, but they were soon followed by a train of laborers of all extractions, though largely Irish, many of them direct from the Emerald Isle. All sects had an eye to the establishment of a church in accordance with their peculiar tenets. It is a fact in history that men of the Congregational belief were the first to inaugurate public religious worship. In the month of April, 1846, the same month that the Essex Company had the first land sale, arrangements were made for a preaching service in the Essex Company's Broadway boarding

THOMAS CLEGG,

Manufacturer of Loom Reeds and Harnesses, also Leather Board; mill on South Canal, Lawrence, Mass. Residence, 33 Prospect St. Has been in Lawrence thirteen years. Born at Rochdale, England, Jan. 8, 1820. At the early age of eleven years he engaged in the trade of reed and harness making, and is therefore familiar with it in every detail. In 1841 he came to this country and located in Andover, and in 1862 he came to this city, engaging in the reed and harness business in 1865. In 1876 he moved to the new mill on the south canal and added the manufacture of leather board to his other rapidly increasing business. Mr. Clegg was a member of the board of aldermen from Ward I, in 1875, 1876 and 1878.

house, where now stands the store of E. W. Pierce. The sermon was delivered by Rev. Silas Curtis, a Freewill Baptist clergyman. During the summer of the same year services were held in the Durant school house, and a Sabbath School was organized by the Congregationalists, and they also made arrangements and commenced the erection of a vestry. The Methodists also commenced to organize that summer and had preaching service one Sabbath.

EPISCOPALS.

The first place of worship was completed for occupancy, and was occupied on the second Sabbath of October that same year, (1846.) It

REV. GEORGE PACKARD.

was where Grace Chapel now stands on Garden street. Rev. George Packard rode over from North Andover that morning and conducted

around us, we may well fear and tremble; looking upward, we have confidence and hope. Upon this and other kindred assurances of our Lord and Master, the Church collectively may, should rest. Our trust is not in an arm of flesh, but in the Lord, mighty and willing to show mercy. We must not lose sight of these promises for good to Zion. We must plead earnestly and perseveringly before the throne, and if we do, having faith, and that faith leading to humble, prayerful, and untiring effort, our experience will be that "*not one good thing hath failed us of all that the Lord hath spoken.*"

Mr. Packard gave notice that a Sunday School would be opened the next Sunday, and on that day, October 18th, there were three teachers and eight scholars. November, 19th, 1846, the church was consecrated under the title of Grace church, by Bishop Eastburn. In ten years more the society had grown so that a new edifice was needed, and the present stone structure was decided on. It was consecrated in May, 1852, by Bishop Eastburn. At that time the walls were uncolored and they remained so till 1860, when they were painted and a window of stained glass put in the chancel. Dr. Packard closed his earthly pilgrimage November 30th, 1876, having completed a thirty years' pastorate of the church. To him the city as well as Grace church is largely indebted. The funeral was largely attended, Bishop Paddock conducting the service. An affecting incident was the presence of two old gentlemen—one named DeRinzey, a resident of the city, almost at death's door himself, the other a colored barber of Ward Six, both having attended the first service Dr. Packard preached in Lawrence.

About a year before Dr. Packard's death, Rev. Wm. Lawrence had been engaged as assistant, and after death, Mr. Lawrence was made rector and still remains in that position. A beautiful memorial window, commemorative of Dr. Packard, has lately been put in the chancel of the church.

St. John's church, now worshipping on Bradford street, began to hold services in the engine house on Morton street. Dr. Packard and others officiating. The church was first built on Morton street on a lot adjoining the engine house. In 1869 the church was removed to Bradford street where it now stands. Its first rector was Prof. Allen, who remained one year, Rev. Mr. Lee four years, and the Rev. Belno A. Brown left this year, after a five years' rectorship, to organize a new church in Methuen. The present rector of St. John's is the Rev. Mr. Wells. About five years ago a surpliced choir was introduced under the distinguished leadership of Mr. Charles Abercrombie, who is now principal tenor at Her Majesty's Chapel Royal. The church building cost about $8,000, which was all subscribed and the edifice consecrated about four years ago by the present Bishop of Massachusetts.

Mr. Frederick Butler who took a very active interest in St. John's church was senior warden until two years ago, when he resigned in favor of Mr. James Walton, the present incumbent. There are now about 250 communicants. A rectory is now in contemplation by the wardens and vestry, and is expected to be built in a very short time on a piece of land adjoining the church.

CONGREGATIONALISTS.

The believers of this faith were first to organize for religious purposes. On the 12th of June, 1846, nine persons petitioned John Tenney, Esq., of Methuen, to issue a warrant calling a meeting to organize a Congregational Society in "Essex City," in Methuen; and on the 8th of August, accordingly, was organized the "Merrimack Congregational Society," since transformed into the Lawrence Street Society, and a house, 44 by 30 feet, was soon after commenced, occupying nearly the site of the present building; this was so far completed as to be occupied for service in December, and was dedicated

JOSEPH SHATTUCK,

Grocer, corner of Essex and Amesbury Streets. Has been in the city since its commencement. Born in Andover, in 1827. Educated at Phillips Academy. Entered the grocery of Josiah Crosby (the first grocery store opened in the town) as clerk, in 1845. Succeeded Mr. Crosby, engaging in business for himself in 1850. A year later he was joined in business by his brother, Charles W., the firm continuing to the present time. Increasing business demanded the building of their present brick block two years ago. Mr. Shattuck is a director of the Bay State National Bank; president of the Essex Savings Bank, and a director of the Lowell & Lawrence R. R. Married Maria Cobb in 1857; has three children. Is at present a member of the board of aldermen, from Ward III.

January 10th, 1847. The next Sunday, Rev. Lyman Whiting, of North Brookfield, preached his first sermon to the new society. The church was organized by an ecclesiastical council April 9th, with twenty-nine members, and on June 16th, Rev. Lyman Whiting was installed pastor. The present house of worship was dedicated October 11th, 1848. Mr. Whiting was dismissed in January 1850, and Rev. Henry M. Storrs, of Braintree, was ordained over the church, January 15th, 1852, and remained its pastor till March 1st, 1855, Rev. George B. Wilcox was pastor from September 24th, 1856, to April 13th, 1859, and Rev. Caleb Ellis Fisher from April 13th, 1859, to October 1874.

Mr. Fisher was pastor over this church fifteen years, the longest term of service rendered by any one clergyman—and to his eminent service the present prosperity of the church is largely due. Next to Dr. Packard he was the most representative minister ever settled in the city. He was earnest in the faith, but his love was as broad as the brotherhood of man. His life-work was here, and soon after he left, his health failed and he lived but a short time.

Rev. Joshua Coit, the present pastor, was installed May 23d, 1874. The present membership of the church is 569. The Sunday school membership is 307.

The Central Congregational Church of Lawrence, was organized Dec. 25, 1849. Rev. H. M. Dexter preached the sermon on that occasion, and Rev. Lyman Whiting, then pastor of the Lawrence Street Church in this place, gave the fellowship of the churches. On the Sabbath following, the new church commenced public religious services in the City Hall, which they continued to occupy until the first Sabbath in August, 1854, when they removed to their new house of worship, a substantial brick building, at the corner of Essex and Appleton streets. On Friday, the 12th of August, 1859, at a little past noon, this new house was destroyed by fire. On the Sabbath following, the congregation assembled in the City Hall, where they continued to worship about four months. The regular services of the church and Sunday school during this period, were uninterrupted; the evening meetings being held in the chapel of Grace Church, on Garden street.

On the 30th of September, seven weeks after the destruction of the former house of worship, the corner stone of a new one was laid with appropriate services, on a lot secured for the purpose on Haverhill street, north of the Common. On the second Sabbath of January, 1860, the congregation met for worship in the basement of their new stone building, which was so arranged as to accommodate them with very slight inconvenience. On the 8th of June, 1860, the whole building was dedicated to the Triune God, a sermon being preached on the occasion by the pastor, Rev. Daniel Tenney, from Haggai, ii: 9.

Rev. Lyman Whiting and Rev. E. Whittlesey first served the church as stated supply. The first pastor was Rev. W. C. Foster, January 16, 1852. February 17, 1857, Rev. Daniel Tenney succeeded him and was followed by Rev. Mr. Cordley, who passed away from earth while in the discharge of his duties here. Rev. W. E. Park was the only pastor between Mr. Cordley and the present pastor, Rev. Geo. H. Ide. The latter was installed November 1, 1876. Number of members 343.

A Sabbath school composed of the children and adult members of the congregation, was early organized, and has uniformly been in a flourishing condition.

In August 1865, a joint meeting of the Lawrence street and Central churches unanimously resolved that a third Congregational church was needed, and on the 30th, ten persons met, proposing to join in the formation of the new church. Wm. A. Russell, Geo. A. Fuller, C. A. Brown, E. E. Foster and B. T. Bourne were appointed a building committee. September 28th it was voted to organize the Eliot church, and on the first day of October the first public service of the

GEORGE SANBORN,

Carpenter, for Essex Company. Residence 99 Bradford street. Has been in Lawrence 33 years, being one of the earliest comers to the "new city," and in the employ of the Essex Company since its organization. Mr. Sanborn was born in Epping, N. H., 1823, and learned the carpenter's trade before coming to this city. Had a common school education. Has a family—wife and two children. Attends Lawrence Street Congregationalist church. Was a member of Common Council 1875–76, and is Alderman from Ward IV the present year.

church was held in the City Hall, Prof. J. H. Thayer, of Andover Theological Seminary preaching. October 4th the church was recognized by council, ground having been broken two days before for the present edifice. The original membership was 32. In June 1866, the church voted to invite Rev. Wm. Franklin Snow, who had been supplying the pulpit for four months, to become its pastor. The house was dedicated September 6th, and on the 13th following Mr. Snow was installed as pastor. His ministry was terminated by death January 11, 1871. During his pastorate the church gained from 42 to 216. On the 28th of April 1871, it was voted to extend to Rev. T. T. Munger a call to be pastor of the church, which was accepted on the 27th of April, and, on the 14th of June following, a council was summoned to install the newly elected pastor, the installation sermon being given by Rev. J. M. Manning, D. D., of the old South church, Boston. Soon after the beginning of the new ministry a society was formed to take charge of the property of the church. On the 20th of January 1875, Mr. Munger resigned the pastorate on account of the illness of his family. The resignation was regretfully accepted, and on the 21st of February 1875, Mr. Munger closed his labors with the Eliot church, a sorrow to a great many people. On the 5th of February 1875, a call was extended to Rev. J. H. Barrows to become pastor of the church. This was accepted and on the 14th of March following, Mr. Barrows began his labors. On the 29th of April he was ordained and installed, Rev. E. K. Alden, D. D., of Boston, preaching the sermon. Mr. Barrows is with the church to-day. The growth of the church has been rapid, having increased from 42 in 1865 to 236. During Mr. Barrows' ministry 102 members have been added. The Sunday School membership is now 215.

The South Congregational church originated in a Sunday School first convened by M. C. Andrews and J. B. Fairfield in a school house on Andover street in 1852. The school was continued till 1857 by the founders. At that time Geo. A. Fuller became connected with it, and it was soon removed to the engine house and then to the passenger room of the Boston and Maine depot, where it was held till its friends built a small chapel which was dedicated in 1859. In 1861 the chapel was enlarged. In 1869 it was again too small and that year the building now occupied was built, being dedicated December 25th. An effort was made to have regular services there, and Prof. Edwards A. Park, of Andover Theological Seminary, began to supply the pulpit in October 1865, continuing to do so for three years. Mr. Fuller left the school in 1866 to join the newly formed Eliot church. To Mr. Fuller's energy is largely due the success of the South Lawrence enterprise. Joel Barnes succeeded Mr. Fuller as superintendent, and was followed by George Hardy, J. K. Cole, and the present superintendent, J. H. Lovett. The church was organized May 18th, 1868, but had no regular pastor till 1873. Rev. James G. Dougherty supplied the desk one year beginning October 1869, and in March 1870, Rev. L. Z. Ferris began a term as acting pastor and continued two years. January 1st, 1873, the present pastor, Rev. Clark Carter, began pastoral duty and was installed January 30th. The church organized with 47 members and now has 98, 65 having joined during Mr. Carter's pastorate. The Sunday School is a flourishing department of the church and numbers about 145.

There are two other Congregational churches in the city. The Tower Hill Congregationalist was organized in 1877. This body of worshippers were organized under the name of Trinity Methodists in 1872, but in a few years it was found that a large majority of the attendants was in full sympathy with the Congregational faith, and accordingly the name of the church was changed. They have no settled minister at present.

On the 9th of March 1878, forty-three out of fifty two worshippers desiring to have the Riverside Sunday School instituted into a Congregational church, a conference was convened that day and the church fully instituted. The pulpit is supplied from the Andover Institution.

LUTHER LADD,

Treasurer and Agent of the Lawrence Lumber Company. Office at Essex Yard. Has been in Lawrence thirty-two years. Was born at Gilmanton, N. H., in 1821. In early life he worked at lumbering and in a saw mill. Engaged with the Lawrence Lumber Company soon after arriving in this city, and has continued his connection with said company ever since. Resides at 9 Morton Street ; his family consists of a wife and two children. Is a regular attendant at the Lawrence Street Congregational Church. Mr. Ladd is one of the directors of the Bay State National Bank ; has been chief engineer of the Lawrence Fire Department seventeen years. Alderman in 1862 and the present year.

BAPTISTS.

Soon after the commencement of active operations by the Essex Company, a few individuals—Ephriam Ward, Jr., Elbridge Weston, Wm. Hardy, Asa H. Gould, J. C. Whitney, Samuel Easter, and S. Lyford, feeling the necessity of establishing their identity as Baptists, consulted together at the house of Samuel Easter. The result was a determination to have occasional preaching from ministers of their own denomination. On Sunday, February 14th, 1847, Rev. Mr. Fitz preached the first sermon to a Baptist congregation, in the "Old School-house," then located near what is now the site of the first Methodist church. Meetings were held and occasional sermons preached, but no definite steps, of which there is any record, were taken, looking to an organization, until March 11th, 1847, when a meeting was held at the house of Mr. Samuel Easter "for the purpose of considering the propriety of forming a Baptist church, and to take measures in regard to erecting a house of worship." Committees were appointed to "deliberate upon the question whether the ownership should be vested in the church or in a society, and to select a site upon which to build." At a subsequent meeting, March 25th, the committee reported in favor of vesting the ownership of all property in a society, and the lot in the rear of the present edifice was selected as a building lot for a temporary house of worship. At this meeting a committee to raise funds to build a house was appointed, and a constitution informally adopted. The first blow was struck upon the temporary house, March 26th, 1847, and was occupied for the first time on the 14th of April. This house was 25 by 40 feet, and was abundantly capacious for the wants of the society at that time. But on the 28th of November, in the same year, the demand for seats could not be supplied, and an addition of twenty-five feet was made to its length. So rapid, however, was the increase of the society that it was found necessary to take immediate steps toward the erection of a permanent house of worship. June 12th, 1849, ground was broken upon the site of the present edifice, which was given to the society by the Essex Company. The basement was finished and occupied on the first Sunday in January, 1850. On the 20th of October, 1850, the house was dedicated to the worship of God, Rev. J. G. Richardson preaching the dedicatory sermon from Psalms, 93 : 5.

Convinced of the necessity of securing the labors of an efficient under-shepherd to watch over the interests of the flock gathered in this young but enterprising city, on the 5th of September the church extended a call to the Rev. J. G. Richardson to become their pastor, which he accepted, and on the 20th of October, he entered upon his labors with them, and was publicly installed as pastor, December 5th, 1847. He remained till July, 1853. December 27th, 1853, Rev. A. W. Sawyer was ordained and installed over the church. He remained two years and three months. In 1856 Rev. Frank Remington was installed, and began his labor on the first of September. Mr. Remington resigned in August 1859, and the pulpit was supplied for some months by Rev. J. Sella Martin. In December 1859, Rev. Henry F. Lane was called. He left in November 1862 to accept the chaplaincy of the 41st (three years) regiment Mass. volunteers. In August, 1863, the next pastor, Rev. George Knox, began his work, and he too left to become chaplain of the 29th Maine regiment. He was killed in Washington by being thrown from his horse. September 1, 1865, Rev. Dr. Geo. W. Bosworth became pastor, remaining three years and four months. He was succeeded by the present pastor, John B. Gough Pidge, who was ordained September 8, 1869.

The Second Baptist church was organized in September, 1860, with 67 members, all from the 1st Baptist church. Rev. Frank Remington was the first pastor. They held services for a few months in the City Hall, when a chapel was purchased of the Christian Baptists on Common street, near where the carriage house connected with

SILAS H. LORING,

Tobacconist, 241 Essex St.; residence 49 Farnham St. Has been in Lawrence 15 years. Born at West Boylston, Mass., Sept. 18, 1833. Received a common school education, and is a mechanic by trade. Married Carrie B. Hyde of Cambridgeport, in 1855; has three sons. Is a Universalist in his church connections. Served as an enlisted man in the 51st Mass. Regiment, in the nine month's service in the department of North Carolina, and was for two years quartermaster of Needham Post, No. 39, G. A. R. Was the only republican member of the board of aldermen in 1877, being elected to fill the vacancy caused by death of Alderman Howard. Mr. Loring took an active interest in offering to the Boston & Lowell Railroad easy access to the city by the new route, and also in the purchase of Den Rock for cemetery purposes. Alderman from Ward VI, the present year.

Stowell & Spalding's stable now stands. This chapel was afterwards moved to the lot of land the church now occupies, enlarged and opened for worship January 11th, 1865. In 1874 the house of worship having become too small for the congregation, the old chapel was torn down and the present church edifice built and opened for worship in November of the same year. The church has had for pastors: Revs. Frank Remington, C. F. Tolman, Henry A. Cooke, L. L. Wood, George W. Gile. The present pastor, Mr. Gile, was settled July 1st, 1873. There have been received into the church since its organization more than one thousand members. Present number, 698.

The Olive Baptist church, (colored) was organized in 1871. Rev. W. H. Garrett has been pastor since its organization. It has a membership of 43.

FREE BAPTISTS.

The organization of this church took place January 17th, 1847, with twelve members. The first pastor was Rev. J. E. Davis, now deceased, who remained with the church about three years, in which time sixty-four members were added. Rev. J. Woodman, known as "Father Woodman," assumed the pastoral charge October 1st, 1849, remaining also about three years, and receiving to the church sixty-six members. In December, 1852, he was succeeded by Rev. G. P. Ramsey, also now deceased, under whose charge sixty-seven were added to the church. In 1855 Mr. Ramsey resigned, and Rev. A. D. Williams was installed as Pastor. Up to this time the church had occupied a small chapel on Haverhill street, corner of White. It was now decided to remove to another site and build larger. Accordingly the lot was exchanged for the present one, and the present church edifice erected and dedicated in the spring of 1857. Rev. E. M. Tappan was pastor from September 1857 to his death in December, 1860. During his pastorate over one hundred members were added. Rev. E. G. Chaddock was pastor for four years from June, 1866, and Rev. J. A. Lovell a year and a half from from October, 1870. The present pastor is Rev. A. L. Houghton. The church membership is 445, of which 244 have been added during Mr. Houghton's pastorate.

UNITARIANS.

The Unitarian church was organized in 1847. The first pastor was Rev. Henry F. Harrington, now superintendent of schools in New Bedford. Mr. Harrington was an active member of the school committee here and did much to give the schools of Lawrence the excellent character they have uniformly maintained. Mr. Harrington was followed by Rev. J. L. Junkins, and he by Rev. J. H. Wiggin who, however, only remained one year. Rev. James B. Moore served several years and was succeeded Rev. C. A. Hayden, who in turn was followed by the present pastor, Rev. E. R. Sanborn. The church was organized under the statutes, and this year, under the present pastor, it has been reorganized in some particulars. There are now departments of public worship and instruction, Sunday School and social and literary culture, fellowship and benevolent work. The number of families now included in the parish is 132.

METHODISTS.

The Haverhill street Methodist Episcopal church began in 1846, in the private house of Charles Barnes, situated on the southwest corner of Broadway and Tremont street. A small number of persons gathered every Sabbath for almost a year under the pastoral care of Rev. James L. Gleason. Before the year closed they rented Concert Hall, Broadway. In the spring of 1847, Rev. L. D. Barrows was sent to be their pastor, and during his ministry of two years the

MICHAEL P. MERRILL,

Assessor; office at City Hall. Residence, 231 Broadway. Has been in Lawrence twenty-one years. Born at Warren, N. H., Dec. 31, 1817. Received a common school education, and worked at farming until 1855. Married Augusta M. Hoytt, May 30, 1841; has three children. Attends the Universalist church. Was selectman in 1851-2. Moderator of town meeting in 1849, 1850, 1851, 1854, 1855, 1856 and 1857. Superintendent of Schools in 1844, 1845, 1846 and 1852. Commissioned captain, 1837; major, 1839; lieutenant-colonel, 1841; colonel, 1844; brigadier-general, 1845; discharged, 1846. Commissioned brigade drill master in 1848. Assessor in 1863-4, and from 1870 to the present. Gen. Merrill was a member of the common council for 1860, and was elected president for that year.

present edifice on the corner of Hampshire and Haverhill streets was built. It was dedicated on the 26th of March 1848, by the pastor Rev. L. D. Barrows, D. D. The following is a list of the pastors of the church: Rev. James L. Gleason, 1846; L. D. Barrows, 1847–48; James Pike, D. D., 1849; Moses Howe, 1850; Samuel Kelley, 1851–52; R. S. Rust, D. D., 1853–54; Jonathan Hall, 1850–56; W. A. McDonald, 1857; F. A. Hughes, 1858; J. H. McCarty, D. D., 1859–60; S. Holman, 1861–62; R. S. Stubbs, 1863; George Dearborn, 1864; L. J. Hall, 1865–66; D. C. Knowles, 1867–68–69; F. Pitcher, 1870–71; L. D. Barrows, D. D., 1872–73–74; D. Stevenson, D. D., 1875–76–77; D. C. Knowles, 1878. The first board of trustees consisted of the following persons: John N. Marble, Alvah Bennett, Rufus C. Barber, Jonathan Russell, Alexander Fife, James K. Barker and J. W. Mathes.

The Garden street Methodist society held its first meeting April 24th, 1853. Rev. George P. Wilson was the superintendent of the Sunday School and Rev. Mr. Hanson the pastor. The church was organized the same year. The records of the society are deficient, and we are unable to present a complete record. Some of the pastors have been Rev. Messrs. Holman, H. H. Hartwell, C. M. Dinsmore, Trueman Carter, C. U. Dunning, E. P. Cushman, E. W. Norris, W. E. Bennett, and the present pastor, A. E. Drew. The church numbers 478 members, with 52 probationers.

The Trinity Methodist church on Haverhill street, was organized January 15th, 1873. Up about this time the members forming this society had been a part of the Free Congregational society, worshipping first on Common street and then on Essex street, that society having grown out of a union mission Sunday School. Later in 1872 the society divided, one part going to form the Tower Hill Union Evangelical church. The remaining twenty-five members were organized by Rev. L. D. Barrows into a Methodist church. They were for some time under the pastoral care of Mr. Barrows, he being then the pastor of the Haverhill Street Methodist Church. March 21st, they completed their organization by the appointment of trustees and stewards. The present edifice on Haverhill street, west of Broadway was built about four years ago. The present pastor, Rev. D. C. Smith, has been with the church about one year.

Parker Street M. E. church, South Side, was organized in 1873. In the year 1869 Rev. D. C. Knowles, of the Haverhill street church conceived the idea of forming a class which at some future time should form the nucleus of a church. Five persons formed the class which met weekly in the Tiger Engine House, on Broadway. The class had a sickly existence for some time, but at length rallied and the members resolved to erect a small structure and organize a church. A society was duly organized September 16th, 1870. A lot of land was purchased on Blanchard street, and the building erected. At this time the society had only eight members. From week to week the congregation gathered in this chapel and were for two years under the spiritual leadership of Rev. Mr. Tilton, of Derry, Rev. Mr. Keys of Woburn, Rev. A. D. Sargent of Malden, and another year by Rev. W. J. Parkinson of Boston. In 1873 the present church edifice was built at a cost of $15,000, since which the church has been supplied by the conference. Rev. Garrett Beekman, 2 years, C. L. McCurdy 1 year, A. J. Hall 1 year, and T. J. Abbott 1 year, dying after a short illness near the close of the year. The present pastor is Rev. W. A. Braman. The church numbers 100 members, with 21 on probation. Sunday School 132 scholars, 18 teachers.

UNIVERSALISTS.

On the 25th of October, 1848, Geo. Littlefield, Sullivan Symonds, Wm. D. Joplin, Heaton Bailey and others issued a manifesto addressed to George A. Waldo, Justice of the Peace, to organize a church of the Universalist faith. The meeting convened and the

ALBERT V. BUGBEE,

City Treasurer. Office at City Hall; residence, 25 Orchard Street. Born at Chelsea, Vt. in 1834. Obtained a limited education, being obliged to earn his own livelihood after he was eleven years of age. Became a citizen of Lawrence in 1852, and was fifteen years in the auction and commission business. Following that he was for eight years in the insurance, auction and real estate business. Elected city treasurer in 1875, from which time to the present he has continued to fill the office. Mr. Bugbee attends the Universalist church. Married Emily S. Johnson of Lowell in 1851, and has two children.

church was organized on November 15th of the same year. Fairfield White, Heaton Bailey, Frederick Tyler, Daniel O. Emerson and Ethel O. Nutters' were elected standing committee. The present church edifice was dedicated June 30th, 1853. The first pastor was Rev. Geo. H. Clark, from 1847 to 1851; Rev. Henry Jewell, 1851–52; Rev. J. R. Johnson, 1852 to 1855; Rev, J. J. Brayton, 1855 to 1858; Rev. M. J. Steere, 1858 to 1860; Rev. G. S. Weaver, 1861 to 1873; Rev. Geo. W. Perry, 1873 to 1877; and succeeded by Rev. A. E. White, the present pastor.

PRESBYTERIANS.

In the month of April, 1854, a few Presbyterians feeling that their wants were not fully met in the Congregational churches, got together at a private residence and held a prayer-meeting, William Adams being chosen to visit the people and ascertain how many were desirous of forming a church. June 30th, following, Rev. A. McWilliams, a licentiate from the Presbytery of Boston, came here and organized a church with 47 members. For two years services were held in the Union School house on Jackson street. In 1856 the church was built on Oak street, and preaching continued a little more than a year when Mr. McWilliams left, the hard times of 1857 and the stoppage of the Bay State Mills tending to greatly weaken the congregation. In 1859 Rev. James Dinsmore was installed and remained until 1862. Meetings were then suspended and the building went into the hands of the Presbytery, it subsequently being let to the city for a school house. In 1867 the worshippers of this faith having largely increased, the church was re-dedicated and Rev. John Hogg called to the pastorate, who remained eight years. Early during his labors the new church on Concord street was built. The pastor during the year 1877 was Rev. John A. Burns, who resigned on account of ill health, and at present the church is without a settled pastor, though a call has been extended to Rev. Mr. McAegal, of Ohio.

For several years the Adventists have sustained a regular church but have had a settled pastor but a small share of the time. They at first had a chapel on Common street, but subsequently removed to Bradford street where religious services are now held.

CATHOLICS.

The early comers to Lawrence included a large Catholic element, and consequently the clergy of that order were active in looking after their interests. In December, 1848, Rev. James O'Donnell erected old St. Mary's church. He established the parochial schools and

REV. JAMES O'DONNELL.

brought the Sisters here. He began his services on the corner of Newbury and Common streets. He labored zealously and effectually, and died April 17th, 1861. He was succeeded by Rev. Ambrose

ST. MARY'S NEW CHURCH.

A. Mullen, who remained from June, 1861, till August, 1866, when he left to take the presidency of Villanova College. He was followed by Rev. L. M. Edge, who erected the new Catholic church, but died before it was completed. Then came Rev. Thomas Galberry, now bishop of the diocese of Hartford, Conn. Rev. John P. Gilmore succeeded Father Galberry, July 2d, 1872. Father Gilmore was born in Philadelphia, October 5th, 1844. The Church of the Immaculate Conception was begun by Father French, who came here from Ireland. He rebuilt the old wooden church of the same name. He was followed by Father Taaffe, who erected the present buildings of the Immaculate Conception, the Orphan Asylum, and organized the Catholic Friends' Society. He died March 29th, 1868, and was followed by Father Michael Dougherty, temporarily, who stayed till the appointment of Rev. William Orr in 1860. Father Orr was succeeded by Rev. J. P. Gilmore in the care of the church, with Rev. D. D. Regan as rector. In July, 1873, the St. Laurence church was opened. Father Gilmore erected the parochial residence on Haverhill street, and opened it October 5th, 1873. It cost $30,000, and Father Gilmore may well congratulate himself that this handsome structure is paid for. The Catholic clergy of Lawrence, north of the river, of which Father Gilmore is the head, are Revs. M. M. O'Farrell, J. H. Devers, J. A. Marsden, and P. C. McGovern, all members of the order of St. Augustine. There are 13,000 Catholic communicants in Lawrence, and an average attendance in the parochial schools of 1000 pupils, 400 boys and 600 girls. Rev. Father Devers has lately come to Lawrence and has been assigned to the Immaculate Conception church. St. Patrick's church in South Lawrence, was begun in 1869, by Father Orr, and was dedicated on the following St. Patrick's Day by Very Rev. Father Lyndon, the lately deceased Vicar-General of the diocese. Father Orr was succeeded by Rev. James Murphy, the present pastor. He is assisted by Rev. James Sheedy.

JAMES ERVING SHEPARD,

City Clerk ; office at City Hall. Residence, 26 Summer Street. Has been in Lawrence ten years. Was born in Union, Me., Jan. 9, 1835 ; received a common school education. Married Abbie Bennett Cooper, April 4, 1864 ; has no children. Attends the Second Baptist church, and is a democrat in politics. Mr. Shepard worked on a farm and at the cooper's trade in his earlier days, and also learned the Daguerrian's art. In 1861 he enlisted as a private in Co. D., 9th Maine Volunteers. Receiving the intermediate promotions he was on July 6th, 1863 made Regimental Adjutant ; served on staff duty till the close of the war. Came to Lawrence in 1868. Was city marshal in 1870. Employed as a newspaper writer for three years. Clerk of the Water Board for 1874, 1875 and 1876. City Clerk for 1877, and re-elected in 1878.

The French Catholics of Lawrence worship in their brick church on Haverhill street, Rev. O. Boucher, pastor. The first movement among the French Catholics here was in December, 1871, when bishop (now archbishop) Williams, asked Father Gearin of Lowell, to come here and see what could be done. Father Gearin was superior of his order. He was assisted by Father Beaudin. They began worship in Essex Hall. In March, 1872, Father Beaudin left and Father Lecompte took charge till October 1st, 1872, when Father Michaud followed him. Father Gearin had bought the chapel on Lowell street early in March, 1872. In Father Michaud's time the society attempted to build their present church edifice, but became considerably involved, and he left in Septembr, 1874. There was no regular pastor till March, 1875, when the present pastor came. The church has about 1300 communicants.

At present there are 28 churches in the city. The two not enumerated above are the Swedenborgian and German Protestant, both without a house of worship and with but few adherents.

VIII.

THE CORPORATIONS.

To compile a history of Lawrence without a detailed description of the corporations would be like the play of Hamlet with Hamlet left out. These are the backbone of the city. They give directly employment to about one third of the population and are the life blood of a goodly majority of the remaining two thirds, as nearly all the wealth and the ready cash in circulation comes through the monthly pay of the operatives of these manufactories. When pay-day arrives, each month on the large corporations 'tis then the grocer, the butcher, the baker,—in fact every retail dealer of merchandise expects to count in the dollars for goods delivered in the interim since last pay-day.

The inception, growth and development of the corporations lining the banks of the river is almost marvelous—outrivalling even the "magic growth" of western cities. It is now thirty-two years since the north canal was completed and work commenced in the construction of the Bay State, now Washington Mills and the Atlantic Mills. From that beginning has sprung up one of the busiest cities in the world, and a population of 40,000 find home and comforts from the manufacturing industries. The corporations as a rule have been very successful. The financial depression of 1857 caused a suspension in nearly all the mills for a short time; then occurred the failure of the Washington Mills and their reorganization. In 1860

BYRON TRUELL,

Dry Goods and Carpet House, 249 Essex St. Residence, 355 Haverhill St. Came to this city in February, 1854, and became merchant's clerk in the store of A. W. Stearns. In 1858, he entered business under the firm name of Bailey & Truell. This partnership was dissolved in 1863, and he has since continued business under the name of Byron Truell & Co., at the present stand. Born at St. Johnsbury, Vt., Nov., 1834. Married in 1859, and has two children. Attends the Haverhill Street M. E. Church. Mr. Truell was State senator in 1877 and 1878, and was in the House in 1875 and 1876. Was in the common council in 1875. Is at present justice of the peace and a director of the Pacific National Bank.

occurred the terrible Pemberton Mills calamity, when the mill fell, burying 700 operatives in the ruins. When the War of the Rebellion broke out in 1861 the great Pacific had fairly regained its feet, and the mills generally were ready for the extensive business that came to their doors.

The managers took an opposite course from that taken by the Lowell manufacturers, for whatever may have been their opinion as to the duration and extent of the war, they believed it policy to work up all the cotton they had, and procure as much as they could in the early days of the strife, and they eagerly sought the raw article placed on the market by the Lowell managers. Subsequent events proved their course to have been wise. During the business depression of the past few years the Lawrence mills and operatives have probably suffered less than those of any other large city. To-day the mills are running to nearly their full capacity, and, with the exception of a few months' stoppage of the Atlantic Mills, during their reorganization, the same is true of all these months of hard times. True, the wages of the operatives have been reduced, and in some cases to a large extent; but work has been provided the people, and while those of other manufacturing centres have suffered for food and clothing, here they have been deprived of but few comforts. Unlike the mills of Fall River, the management of all the Lawrence mills is centred in Boston, and the leading officials are unknown to the people. The only irregularity of any magnitude ever occurring in the Lawrence mills was the recent defalcation of George R. Waterman, head clerk of the local management of the Pacific Mills, who, in a systematic manner for 55 months, stole an amount averaging $2000 per month, aggregating $110,000. For this skillfully planned theft he is now serving a twelve years' sentence in the State Prison at Concord. Since their incorporation there have been serious reverses, and reorganizations of the Pacific, Atlantic, Washington and Pemberton Mills.

The present aggregated statistics of the seven leading manufactories are as follows:

Capital stock	$7,350,000
Number of spindles	338,100
Number of looms	9,057
Males employed	4,200
Females employed	6,000
Yards produced per week	2,301,654

The average wages earned by men and boys are $1.30 per day; by women and girls, 90 cents per day.

To show the comparative value of the manufacturing corporations and the share of the burden they carry in the way of aid towards municipal development, the amount of taxes levied by the city assessors for the current year is here given. The rate of taxation is $15 per thousand dollars' valuation.

Atlantic Cotton Mills	$19,855 00
Arlington Mills	5,250 00
Archibald Wheel Co	480 00
Essex Company	10,875 00
Everett Mills	10,200 00
Lawrence Duck Co	3,375 00
Lawrence Flyer and Spindle Co	624 00
Lawrence Gas Co	5,625 00
Lawrence Lumber Co	615 00
Lawrence Woolen Co	2,175 00
Pemberton Co	8,700 00
Pacific Mills	57,750 00
Russell Paper Co	2,400 00
Washington Mills	20,055 00
Wright Manufacturing Co	705 00

LEVI EMERY,

Farmer, owning a farm of sixty acres overlooking the city from the west. Born in Salem, N. H., August, 1818; worked on a farm in early life; afterwards spent six years at shoe manufacturing in Malden. Was for several years in the West, near Chicago, acting during the time as agent for the Tremont Land Co., and instituting many improvements in drainage and agriculture in that section. Came to Lawrence in 1864 and purchased the estate upon which he now resides. Mr. Emery is married and has one child. Attends the Eliot Congregational church. Was in the common council in 1867, 1868, 1872, 1875 and 1876, and a member of the legislatures of 1877-8.

WASHINGTON MILLS.

The Washington Mills were the first built in the town of "Merrimack," as Lawrence was then known. The mills were built in 1846, and put in operation the following year, under the name of the Bay State Mills. There are three large brick buildings, each like the other, comprising, with the roof or attic, nine stories. The departments of manufacture are woolen, worsted and cotton goods. In the financial crash of 1857, the mills were shut down, and, in 1859, started under a reorganization, the corporate name being Washington Mills. The famous Bay State shawls, and blue flannel coatings, were originated by these mills, the former in 1848, the latter in 1859; opera flannels were also first introduced in this country by these mills. The works are the most extensive in the manufacture of a general range of woolen goods of any in this or any other country. In 1868 was commenced the manufacture of worsted coatings, through the influence of the managing director, Hon. E. R. Mudge, who was United States Commissioner at the Paris Exposition in 1867, and there became convinced of the feasibility of such manufacture in this country. From the beginning the corporation has conducted operations on an extended scale, and at the present time its various fabrics not only stand without equal in this country, but fully equal similar productions in Europe. Throughout the recent financial stress the greater portion of the machinery has been kept running, though the depression in the wool market has had a serious effect upon the profits. The first president was Mr. E. A. Bourne, who retired in 1862, when Joseph S. Fay succeeded him, remaining but two years; John A. Blanchard followed, and in 1866, George M. Minot assumed the position, remaining till 1872, when the present incumbent, P. T. Homer, accepted the office. Joseph S. Fay was treasurer, resigning in 1862, followed by Joshua Stetson, who retired in 1868, on account of ill health. The position remained vacant for a year, when the present treasurer, Henry F. Coe, was elected. The board of directors comprises P. T. Homer, E. R. Mudge, Henry Saltonstall, C. U. Cotting, C. W. Freeland, Robert Couch and J. A. Blanchard, Jr. The statistics show that there are one cotton, one worsted, and five woolen mills, with 19,000 cotton spindles, 65 sets cards, 320 broad looms; worsted department, 8640 spindles, 885 looms; the weekly product is 100,000 yards cottons, 120,000 yards dress goods, 20,000 yards worsteds, 40,000 yards woolens and 1000 shawls; pounds cotton consumed, 728,000; clean woolen and worsted stock, 30,000; tons coal per year, 10,000; gallons oil per year, 24,000; pounds starch, 23,500; motive power, 7 water wheels of 1025 horse power, and two engines of 1,000 horse power. The capital stock of the mill is $1,650,000. Females employed, 1268; males, 1135.

Peter T. Homer, President; Henry F. Coe, Treasurer; E. R. Mudge, Henry Saltonstall, Robert Couch, John Saltonstall among the directors. Robert Scott, Agent; A. P. Clark, Paymaster; G. M. Stoddard, Superintendent Worsted Department; James B. Siner, Mechanical Superintendent; Frank Atkins, Superintendent of Cotton and Woolen Department.

Assets.

Real estate, land and water power, buildings, machinery,	$1,373,634 83
Cash and debts receivable	351,332 22
Manufactures, material and stock in process	1,680,605 19
Total	$3,405,572 24

Liabilities.

Capital stock	$1,650,000 00
Debts, including dividend declared payable Jan. 1	1,454,538 75
Reserves	138,935 60
Balance profit and loss	162,097 89
Total	$3,405,072 24

GRANVILLE M. STODDARD,

Superintendent of the Washington Mills. Residence, 28 Washington Corporation. Born at Dover, Me., in 1839, and removed with his father's family to this city in 1847. Entered upon the realities of life by learning the apothecary's business with Dr. Smith, formerly on Merchants' Row. He also worked at the same business for some years in Boston. Mr. Stoddard has been in the employ of the Washington Mills Corporation for the past twenty years; two years in the office, then in the embossing room, and afterwards in the worsted department. He has been superintendent the past six years. Married Laura J. Stockman in 1868; has two children. Attends the Unitarian Church.

ATLANTIC MILLS.

The Atlantic Mills were the second in operation in Lawrence, the building of which began in 1846, but a few months after the Bay State Mills. The original capital was $1,800,000, and the present capital is $1,000,000. Originally it was intended to erect four large mills, each with a capacity of 12,500 spindles and 1466 looms, and to occupy all the space between the Pacific and Bay State Mills; the plan was modified, and but two mills were erected, running 25,000 spindles and 733 looms. Mills commenced operation in 1849. In 1852 a large centre mill was built, connecting the two wings, making a mammoth structure. These mills have had failures and successes, and in 1876 approached a crisis, which resulted in a general reorganization, and of so recent a date as to be familiar to the reader of to-day. In brief, the treasurer, William Gray of Boston, a very extensive owner, and, also, the selling agent of the mills, refused to longer indorse the corporation paper. During that year the stock went down to $18 per share. In July it was decided to reorganize, and the capital of $1,000,000 was scaled down to $300.000, and new created sufficient to make a capital of $1,000,000. An old stockholder was privileged to exchange five of the old shares for one of the new, and to take a proportional part of the new stock.

The mills remained idle from June to September, during which time there was much grumbling by the stockholders, many of whom failed to relish the fact that Mr. Gray, as treasurer and selling agent, was drawing a princely salary and handsome profits. A strong effort was made to remove the local agent, Mr. J. P. Battles, but without success. Mr. Gray resigned in July, and the mills renewed work in September, 1876, under the treasurership of Henry Saltonstall, who was also treasurer of the Chicopee Manufacturing company. Wm. Gray & Son retired from the selling agency, and the goods now pass through the house of E. R. Mudge, Sawyer & Co. At the annual meeting in 1877 William Gray, Jr., was elected treasurer. Since the reorganization the mills have prospered fairly, and the stock has attained a handsome figure above par. The new Boston and Lowell railroad has cut through the mill yard and the corporation boarding houses, but it is believed by many that the entrance of this road will prove advantageous rather than detrimental to its interests. The products of the mills are white goods exclusively—shirtings and sheetings, which are of very excellent quality. There are three mills, 87,888 spindles, 1804 looms, 1040 employes; 17,000 bales of cotton are used, and 23,200,000 yards of cloth made annually; oil, 6000 gallons; coal, 3000 tons; motive power, one steam engine of 500 horse power, and four turbine water wheels.

Charles H. Dalton, President; Wm. Gray, Jr., Treasurer; Charles H. Dalton, William Gray, Jr., and Henry Saltonstall among the Directors. J. P. Battles, agent; J. C. Bowker, paymaster.

Assets.

Real estate, land and water power, buildings, machinery,	$950,992 41
Cash and debts receivable	150,349 41
Manufactures, material and stock in process	372,924 09
Miscellaneous	21,722 06
Total	$1,495,987 97

Liabilities.

Capital stock	$994,844 45
Debts	489,383 82
Balance profit and loss	7,872 80
Reserve unpaid bills	3,886 90
Total	$1,495,987 97

PACIFIC MILLS.

The Pacific Mills are the most extensive works of the kind in the world. Within the yards used for manufacturing purposes are twelve

ALBERT R. FIELD,

Superintendent of Pacific Mills; residence, 4 Concord St. Has been in Lawrence since 1871. Born in Cranston, R. I., in the year 1821. Received a common school education. Commenced work in the mill at an early age. In 1849 he commenced running a small mill in Scituate, R. I., under the firm name of Ralph & Field. In 1860 received the appointment of agent of the Anthony Mills, Coventry, R. I. In 1864 removed to Harrisville, and took charge of the Harris Manuf'g Co., purchasing a half interest in the mills. In 1867 was temporarily employed starting up the Duval Mills, Fall River. Moved the same year to Central Falls, R. I., taking the agency of N. W. Sprague's new mill for the manufacture of fine lawn goods. Resigned to accept present position in 1871. Married Abby C. Johnson in 1860; has two children. Was a member of the Board of Aldermen in 1877, and is a member of the present Water Board.

mills and buildings, affording 41 acres of flooring. There are 5360 people are employed, and it may be said that more than one third of the population of Lawrence are directly dependent upon these mills for their daily bread. The Pacific was incorporated in 1852, with a capital of $2,000,000, and, considering the gloomy aspect at its start, with a probable failure staring its stockholders in the face during the first few years, its career of success has been wonderful. The par value of the stock is $1000, and within 20 years its market value has gone from as low as $75 up to over $2000 a share, and, under the present depressed times is selling in the vicinity of $1850. The construction of the works cost more than the $2,000,000 of original capital; but the corporation was saved from a failure by the munificence of its president, the Hon. Abbott Lawrence, who, from his private fortune, contributed several hundred thousands of dollars, which tided the corporation over the emergency. Until "hard times" came, in 1857, some money was made, but the enterprise was largely sustained by borrowing; in that year the Pacific was forced to ask an extension of credit, which was granted by every creditor. During that year the stock sank as low as $75; and here it may be said that several Lawrence gentlemen of present wealth may date the beginning of their road to fortune from the time when they had means and courage to buy a few shares of Pacific stock. In 1858, the stockholders were called upon to increase the capital to $2,500,000. Matters proceeded fairly until 1859, when the corporation lost money, but, since that time, an unprecedented success has attended the running of these vast mills, its stock has doubled its par value in the market, and very handsome dividends are declared. In 1860 the annual product was 11,000,000 yards of dress goods; in 1870 the product reached 45,000,000 yards, and since then the product, with the cloths purchased of other mills and printed here, has reached 65,000,000—sufficient to put a bandage three-quarters of a yard wide once and a half around the world. For many years the local agent was Mr. Chapin, assisted by A. M. Wade, as superintendent; but several years ago a change was effected, and Mr. John Fallon, formerly in charge of the printing department, was made acting agent, and Mr. A. R. Field, assistant. Apparently the mills were never in a more thriving condition. The grand success of the corporation is, without doubt, to be attributed to the admirable management of Hon. J. Wiley Edmands, lately deceased, allied with the mercantile sagacity of Mr. James L. Little, as the selling agent, and whose creative taste has been imparted to all the fabrics of these mills. The company has a world-wide reputation for its attention to the moral, social and sanitary condition of its employes, which is shown from its support of a vast library and reading room, its benefits to the sick and injured, its cleanliness in its boarding houses, and in aiding employes to build for themselves comfortable homes.

It is within bounds to state that more than forty per cent. of the heads of families own their homes, the company in many instances having assisted their operatives by loaning them money at 6 per cent. wherewith to build houses. To encourage economy among the laborers a savings bank was established years ago whereby the females and minors can, if they choose, deposit a part of their earnings each month, which is put at interest at time of deposit. For prudential reasons the operations of this method of receiving deposits has been considerably curtailed of late, but to some extent it is still in force.

The Pacific Mills Relief Society is an institution of itself worthy of a place in history. The society as its name indicates, was formed for the purpose of extending aid to the sick and to those who meet with accident while there employed. The funds of the society are created as follows: The corporation pays $2.50 weekly, and each person in the employ of the corporation if they receive more than three dollars per week for wages, two cents per week. If less than three dollars wages, one cent per week.

JOSIAH CLINTON WHITE,

Master Mechanic at the Pacific Print Works. Resides at 31 Pacific Corporation. Has been in Lawrence thirty-one years. Was born in Brattleboro, Vt,, July 9, 1828. Learned the carpenter's trade of his father in Brattleboro. Went to Nashua, N. H. in April, 1846, and worked at his trade until September of that year, when he came to the new city, "Andover Bridge," which has since been his home. Was married Jan. 1, 1855 to Edna A. Underwood of Swanzey, N. H.; has two daughters. He is a member of the Eliot Congregational church. Captain White enlisted in Co. G, 30th Mass. Reg't, Oct. 1861. Was wounded while on provost duty at New Orleans, La., May 18, 1862. May 18, 1863, commissioned captain by the President of the United States. Was wounded at the battle of Hovey Hill, Nov. 30th, 1864. Received an honorable discharge from the army May 29th, 1866. Was a member of the common council for 1877; re-elected for 1878.

The officers of this society are a President, Treasurer, and Secretary, with twenty-five managers, chosen annually the first week in April, from the members. These, together, compose a Board of Government; decide points of dispute, and manage the internal affairs of the Society. The weekly allowance to sick members is as follows:

To those who contribute two cents a week.............$2.00

To those who contribute one cent a week.............. 1.25

The allowance to sick members may continue ten weeks; it shall then be reduced one-fourth, and may be extended twenty weeks longer, should sickness continue. At the end of thirty weeks the allowance shall cease entirely, and shall not be renewed within twelve months.

For the past year the amount paid into this fund is over $8000, over five thousand of which has been spent in the manner above indicated. One thousand francs were awarded to the Pacific Mills at the Paris Exposition, for the admirable manner in which this relief system was conducted.

The corporation boarding houses are a model of neatness and order. The bill of fare from every standpoint is better than the average well-to-do families; the price charged is only $2.25 a week for females and a dollar more for males. Vital statistics show that the rate per cent. of sickness and mortality in the Pacific Mills is less than any other community of like number in the known world.

One glances at the mill statistics with wonderment. Number of cotton spindles, 135,000; worsted spindles, 25,000; looms, 4,500; pounds of cotton used per week, 116,000; pounds of wool, 65,000; yards of cloth printed or dyed each week, over 1,260,000; tons of coal per year, 23,000; steam boilers of 3000-horse power, 50; steam engines of 1200-horse power, 37; turbine water wheels, 2000-horse power, 11; gas burners number 5000, and the cost of gas for the six months used is $30,000; monthly pay-roll, $150,000, the women and girls averaging daily 98 cents, and men and boys, $1.40; women and girls employed, 3,534; men and boys 1,766; total number employes, 5,300; number of houses for work people, 275. The annual cost of raw material for dyeing is over $400,000. The wool consumed each week requires the fleeces of 10,000 sheep. The products of the mills are lawns, percales, and a general variety of dress goods.

The local officers are: John Fallon, agent; A. R. Field, superintendent; John R. Rollins, paymaster; Samuel Barlow, superintendent of print works; Joseph Walworth, superintendent of worsted department. Abbott Lawrence, president; James L. Little, treasurer; J. Huntington Wolcott, Augustus Lowell, Benjamin E. Bates, John M. Little, Arthur T. Lyman, directors.

Assets.

Real estate, water power and machinery	$1,450,000 00
Other assets	1,191,754 12
Manufactures, material, etc	3,337,612 08
Miscellaneous	20,000 00
Total	$5,999,366 20

Liabilities.

Capital stock	$2,500,000 00
Debts	2,078,533 94
Reserves	1,420,812 26
Total	$5,999,366 20

PEMBERTON MILLS.

The Pemberton Mills were incorporated in 1852 by an organization of which J. A. Lowell was the principal owner and the moving spirit. J. Pickering Plummer was the President, and John E. Chase local agent. In 1854 the corporation failed, and was sold at auction to David Nevins, of Methuen, and George Howe, of Boston, for

MICHAEL RINN,

Bookseller and Stationer, 143 Essex St.; residence, 40 Oak St. Has been in Lawrence twenty-eight years. Born in Ireland in 1847, he came to Lawrence when three years of age and was educated in the public schools of the city. Commenced work in the mill at an early age and was severely injured at the fall of the Pemberton Mill, January 10th, 1860. Subsequently he worked in the Washington Mills packing room for seven years, after which he went to learn wool-sorting, which he left to enter his present business. Mr. Rinn is not married; is a Roman Catholic, attending St. Laurence church, and in politics is a democrat. Was elected to the common council from Ward II in 1877; represented the Twentieth District in the legislature in 1878.

$300,000, or about one half its actual value. The Legislature of 1857–58 granted an act of incorporation, and the "Pemberton Manufacturing Company" began operations at once with Mr. Howe as treasurer and Mr. Chase as agent. January 10th, 1860, occurred the terrible catastrophe of the falling and burning of the mill, accompanied with a fearful loss of life. The ruins were sold at auction and bought by Mr. Nevins, who at once reorganized the "Pemberton Company," taking himself more than half of the capital stock of $450,000, the other large owners being George Blackburn and Eben Sutton. The new mill was built on the site of the old one, and started in 1861 with Henry S. Shaw as treasurer, and Mr. Chase as agent. In June of the same year Mr. Chase resigned, and Fred E. Clarke was appointed agent. The officers and management of the mill, since it was rebuilt and reorganized, have not changed. Since Mr. Nevins' first purchase, in 1857, he has been the managing director. He also owns a cotton mill in Methuen, of which Mr. Clarke is also agent. The Pemberton is admirably managed. Its product is mainly confined to cottonades, cotton flannels, ticking cottons, fancy cassimeres, repellents, wool sackings and carriage linings. The statistics of the corporation are as follows: capital stock, $450,000; number of mills two; cotton spindles, 28,060; sets woolen machinery, 14; looms, 669; females employed, 650; males employed, 225; yards made per week, 120,000; pounds cotton consumed per week, 40,000; pounds clean wool consumed per week, 6000; tons of coal per annum, 2200; gallons of oil, 5600; pounds starch, 25,000; water wheels, 3; each 200 horse-power; steam double engines, 300 horse-power.

David Nevins, President; H. S. Shaw, Treasurer; David Nevins, Jr., among the Directors.

Assets.

Real estate, land and water power, buildings and machinery $462,081 45

Other assets	177,764 30
Manufactures, material and stock in process	521,205 69
Total	$1,161,051 44

Liabilities.

Capital stock	$450,000 00
Debts	229,793 45
Balance profit and loss reserve for depreciation,	481,254 99
Total	$1,161,051 44

LAWRENCE DUCK COMPANY.

The Lawrence Duck Company was incorporated in 1853, the original stockholders being three Boston men, Albert Fearing, who was president, now dead, Isaac Thatcher, who has been treasurer from its organization to the present time, and David Whiton, who was clerk until four years ago. Mr. Fearing's stock was distributed to his heirs and a large portion to literary institutions. The capital of the corporation is $300,000, and the product comprises cotton duck for sails and tents, mining duck, used for water courses in the mines, cotton dryer felting for paper mills, and sail twine. Five years ago the mill was enlarged to double its capacity, but the dullness of shipping has kept the product of the mill within its old limits, and now but 150 hands are employed. The corporation has a large trade in mining duck with California and Australia, and prides itself upon the quality of its sail cloth, which was selected in preference to others for Astor's yacht. The burden of management has from the beginning been upon the treasurer, Mr. Thatcher, and the local agent, Mr. Isaac Hayden, both of whom have held their positions for 25 years. Nearly all the machinery used was designed and built under the direction of Mr. Hayden. Aaron Hobert, Jr., of Boston, is the president, and Francis G. Davis of Boston, selling agent.

Aaron Hobart, Jr., President; Isaac Thatcher, Treasurer.

LURANDUS BEACH, Jr.

Was born in Dover, N.,H., Nov. 4, 1832. At the early age of sixteen, Mar. 28, 1848, he entered into partnership with his father in Lawrence, Mass., in the manufacture of Soaps. For some two years after entering business he continued at school, at the same time conducting the business, his father meanwhile remaining in Dover. The partnership was continued for 28 years, until 1876, when L. Beach retired, since he has conducted the business alone in Lawrence and Haverhill, Mass., under the name of Beach Soap Co., Lawrence and L. Beach, Jr., Haverhill. About 1860 he purchased the soap factory at Dover, N. H., which has been conducted under the firm name of L. Beach, Jr., & Co. The soap made under his supervision has gained a world-wide reputation for excellence. Was elected the Lawrence Common Council for 1863, and alderman for the year 1876, Married Miss Persis A. Miller, of Middletown, Conn., 1855, has one child, and is a member of the Haverhill Street M. E. Church.

Assets.

Real estate	$136,474 46
Land and water power	28,288 08
Machinery	149,386 87
Other assets	747 35
Cash and debts receivable	90,983 27
Manufactures and material	81,216 82
Profit and loss	27,656 06
Total	$514,749 91

Liabilities.

Capital stock	$300,000 00
Debts	214,749 91
Total	$514,749 91

EVERETT MILLS.

The Everett Mills were incorporated in 1860, and commenced operations the same year in the large stone machine shop formerly owned by the Essex Company, the corporation purchasing the buildings and eighteen acres of land. The old buildings were extensively altered and repaired, and new structures erected, and first-class machinery placed therein, suitable for the manufacture of a general variety of colored cotton goods; later, machinery was secured for the manufacture of worsted fabrics. The machinery was first put in operation January 1st, 1861. The original capital was $500,000, but six months later it was increased to $700,000, and in December, 1862, another $100,000 was added. Extensive dye-houses and a bleachery are attached to the mills. The products are cottonades, ticks, denims, cheviot shirtings, ginghams, duck, and an extensive variety of dress goods of very excellent quality. At the Centennial Exhibition the mills were awarded a prize, and "commended for excellence in subdued coloring, smoothness of fabrics, general good taste in design of cheviot shirtings. Cottonades of very good quality." The statistics of the mills show 33,280 spindles, 841 looms, 750 employes, and an annual production of 8,000,000 yards of goods, consuming 2,500,000 pounds of cotton. Three thousand tons of coal, 4000 gallons of oil and 45,000 pounds of starch are used annually, and the motive power is furnished by three turbine water wheels. The principal incorporators of the mills were James Dana, Samuel Batchelder, and Chas. W. Cartwright. The first treasurer was Samuel Batchelder of Cambridge, who held the position until 1870, then retiring on account of advanced age; he is now living in Cambridge, and is over 90 years old. His successor was H. Temple, of Boston, who, on account of ill health and the cares of his position as treasurer of the York Mills, of Saco, remained but one year. From 1871 to June 1878, D. D. Crombie, who was local agent under Batchelder, was treasurer. The directors are all prominent business men, who manifest a zealous interest in the management of the details of the mills. The present board comprises Thomas Wigglesworth, Jas. Longley, Abijah E. Hildreth, Augustus Lowell, Abbott Lawrence, Thomas Minns, and James Ellison. At least one member, James Ellison (and perhaps Thomas Wigglesworth), has been in the board since the mills were incorporated. The first agent was the late treasurer, Mr. Crombie, who retired in February 1866, and was succeeded by John R. Perry, who was removed to make place for D. M. Ayer. The vibration of Mr. Crombie from agent to treasurer, and the consequent changes of agents, did not occur without some unpleasantness among some of the management. The necessity for a greater production of goods, in a more economical manner, is supposed to have been the cause of the next change of agents, which occurred three years ago, when Mr. Charles McDuffie, the present incumbent was appointed. The advancement of the market value of the stock

THOMAS A. EMMONS,

Loom Harness manufacturer, 7 May street; residence, 119 May St. Came to Lawrence 11 years ago. Born at Kennebunkport, Me., in 1827. Learned his trade at Biddeford, Me., 28 years ago and has worked at it ever since. Commenced business about 25 years ago at Holyoke, where he remained till 1861. Married Elizabeth Benson at Holyoke in 1853. Has three sons. Attends Second Baptist Church. He erected his mill nine years ago on May street. It was partially destroyed by fire two years ago, and immediately re-built with an additional story.

is certainly an outside evidence that the desired result was attained. The par value of the stock is $100, and the highest quotation ever reached, was $180, in 1864; the lowest $70, in 1875; since the present agent's management the stock has gone up to $88 1-2. Mr. McDuffie has kept the property in prime condition and made many repairs and alterations. A fire occurred last winter which destroyed a large portion of the dye works, but in a few weeks the damage was repaired. With business as good as it has been during the past two years, there is no reason why the stock should not soon touch par value and semi-annual dividends of 3 per cent. be declared. The products of the Everett Mills find a market in the United States and Dominion of Canada. The mills are now running closer to the market consumption than at any time during the past year. George C. Richardson & Co., are selling agents in Boston and New York.

James Longley, President; Eugene H. Samson, Treasurer; Augustus Lowell, Abbott Lawrence, Thomas Minns, A. E. Hildreth, and James Ellison, Directors; Charles D. McDuffie, Agent; William A. Barrell, Paymaster.

Assets.

Land, water power, buildings	$367,000 00
Machinery	373,000 00
Cash and debts receivable	346,763 85
Manufactures, material and stock in process	324,769 25
Total	$1,411,533 10

Liabilities.

Capital stock	$800,000 00
Debts	570,000 00
Reserves	41,533 10
Total	$1,411,533 10

LAWRENCE WOOLEN COMPANY.

The Lawrence Woolen Company was incorporated in war times, 1864, and its projector and principal founder was Capt. O. H. Perry, who is also the head of the house of Perry, Wendell & Fay, Boston, the selling agents of the mills. George P. Upham of Boston, is treasurer, and Captain Perry is the local agent, residing in Andover, and frequently visiting the mill. The corporation has, in a financial view, been straight from its incorporation, though, like other manufactories, especially of woolen goods, it has suffered considerably from the business depression, but is at present "holding its own." The corporation has a capital stock of $150,000, runs one mill of 3280 spindles and 47 looms, employs 125 hands, and manufactures 240,000 yards of woolens per annum, from 156,000 pounds clean wool. The power is furnished by one four-foot water wheel. The products are all kinds of fancy woolen goods for men's and women's wear, especially for cloakings. A specialty is also made of fine woolen shawls, which are manufactured in great variety.

ARLINGTON MILLS.

The Arlington Mills are the youngest of our larger manufacturing establishments, and during their thirteen years' existence have won a brilliant reputation. The act of incorporation was secured in 1865 by Messrs. Robert M. Bailey, Charles A. Lombard, Joseph Nickerson and George C. Bosson, who comprised the stockholders, and the mills were started with a capital of $200,000. The original name was "Arlington Woolen Mills," and the early products were only fancy shirting flannels and wool felted fabrics. In 1866 the buildings were totally destroyed by fire, but rebuilt the following year, when the capital was increased to $240,000. The tariff of 1866, which had given a stimulus to the worsted industry, encouraged the management to embark in the manufacture of women's worsted and cotton

JOHN K. NORWOOD,

Insurance, Real Estate, Loans, &c. Office 6 Lawrence St.: residence 62 Eutaw Street. Has been in Lawrence 21 years. Born at Eastport, Me., August, 1837. Common School education. Worked in dry goods store in early life. Has been in insurance business 12 years. In the war for the Union he served in the 9th Massachusetts Battery three years. Received bullet wound in the right lung at Gettysburg. Mr. Norwood represents in his insurance business, the Phœnix, N. Y.; Fire Association, Pa.; Merchants and American, Newark; Girard, Pa.; Phœnix Life, Hartford; and Citizens and Merrimac, Dwelling House Mutuals with combined assets of $20,785,-787.63. Losses have been paid to the following parties: J. Stowell, D. Saunders, D. Spurr, L. Ladd, Briggs & Allyn, A. Ordway, A. J. French, J. Killalee, Steel & McDonald, H. Plummer, J. Gaffney, G. W. Hills, Essex Co., M. S. Dodge, T. Wilkinson and others to the amount of $65,000.

dress goods, for which a large quantity of new and modern machinery was secured. Many difficulties were encountered in establishing the new enterprise, and less determined men would have become disheartened and abandoned the venture. In 1869 the company became financially embarassed, but the stockholders paid into the treasury the whole amount of the capital, $240,000; a change in management was also made, by the election of Joseph Nickerson for president, and William Whitman for treasurer and general agent.

The local managers are Samuel Smith, superintendent, Chas. Wainwright, cashier. In 1871 began the work of remodelling and increasing the productive capacity of the works, and since then there have been large additions of machinery and buildings. In 1875 the Legislature changed the name to "Arlington Mills," dropping the word "Woolen;" in 1876 the capital was increased to $320,000, and in 1877 again increased to $500,000. To the treasurer, Wm. Whitman, and the local superintendent, Samuel Smith, the corporation is largely indebted for its success, which is now at its high tide. The capacity of the mills for the manufacture of worsted and dress goods is being largely increased the present year by the erection of a dye house, giving three times the capacity for coloring, the mills have had heretofore. To do this required the re-location of the canal, but by the aid of the big Corliss engine the mills have been kept continually running.

One feature has been adopted at these mills that is of great advantage to the operatives, and that is the weekly payment of the help. Every employe of the corporation receives his or her pay every Saturday night,—a plan that might with advantage be adopted by every corporation in the city.

The products of the mills are, especially, black alpacas, mohairs and brilliantines, a class of goods these mills were the first in this country to successfully manufacture, and which it was believed could not be successfully made elsewhere than in Bradford, England; but the

Arlington has fully demonstrated that they can be made in the United States quite equal if not superior in every respect to the fabrics made in Europe. The award for these goods at the Centennial Exhibition was accompanied by a very flattering commendation. The corporation has two mills, 6336 spindles, 508 looms, employs 350 females and 232 males; 5200 pounds of cotton yarn, and 13,000 pounds of clean wool are used weekly, and each week 100,000 yards of goods are manufactured and dyed; 2200 tons of coal and 3800 gallons of oil are used per annum; the motive power is supplied by three Swaine water wheels of 200 horse power, and one Corliss engine of 300 horse power. The help employed is of a superior class, and the utmost harmony exists between the management and employes. The selling agents of the mill are Lawrence & Co.,.Boston, and Thomas T. Lea & Co., Philadelphia.

WRIGHT MANUFACTURING COMPANY.

The Wright Manufacturing Company was incorporated in 1873, the incorporators being A. W. Stearns, A. S. Wright, and A. J. French. For some time the manufacture was largely confined to cotton and alpaca braids, but a little more than two years ago this corporation introduced the manufacture of fine mohair braids, and by processes of their own invention, they are enabled to produce the finest and nicest braids of the world, and at prices that defy competition. The enterprise has been one of marked success from the beginning. They make every variety of pure mohair for trimming and binding, from one to twelve fil, and widths from two to twenty-four lines. About one-half the production of the mill is at present mohair goods.

The capital of the company is $60,000. There are 125 hands employed, and an annual production of goods amounting to about $350,000. The officers at present are A. J. French, President; A. W. Stearns, Treasurer and selling agent. Directors: A. W. Stearns, A. S. Wright, C. W. Stevens; Clerk, Wm. L. Wardman.

CHARLES RUSSELL MASON,

Of the firm of Chas R. Mason & Co., Hardware Dealers, 327 Essex Street, his brother Eugene J. Mason being the other member of the firm, which has been a successful one for many years. Mr. Mason came to this city twenty-three years ago, and established the business in which he is still engaged. He resides at 265 Haverhill Street, and has a family. Born at Cambridge, Mass., March 22, 1832.

These nine embrace all the concerns doing business as corporations in the manufacture of cotton and woolen fabrics within the city limits. All of them derive their chief power from the waters of the Merrimack, with the exception of two, the Everett Mills and the Arlington Mills, these being upon the Spicket river. Water supplies the cheapest motive power for the manufacture of cloths, but from the introduction of steam engines in all the principal mills, some of them of sufficient power to drive the whole works, it is patent that both agencies are necessary for the greatest success.

IX.

MUNICIPAL ADMINISTRATION.

---

* This chapter is devoted to a brief epitome of the political history of Lawrence, not that anything startling or out of the common course has occurred, but for the reason that no fair estimate can be made of the growth and stability of any municipality without some knowledge of how its public trusts have been administered. In common with other municipalities, Lawrence has sometimes felt the ill effects of substituting Policy for Principle. Too frequently men poorly calculated by nature or education for public trusts have been elected to public stations; but as a general thing the government of the town and city has been wisely administered. Perhaps in no city in the Commonwealth have political parties been more evenly divided than in Lawrence. The soil has been almost invariably barren for the growth of any party outside of the two great national divisions, Republican and Democrat. The Labor Reform party, as a party, had a brief existence, because one or both of the great divisions adopted its chief principles. The Prohibitory party has had an existence since prohibition became an issue; but at best its growth has been slow and it has failed to mark its impress, or make its influence felt to any great degree. Not that its supporters were not honest in their belief or earnest in its application, but because the general sentiments of the public and the principles of their professions were not in accord. "Knownothingism," like the measles or any other

* We are indebted to City Clerk J. E. Shepard for information contained in this chapter.

JOHN CALVIN DOW,

Crockery and Plated Ware, 302 Essex St.; residence, 9 East Haverhill St. Came to Lawrence April 20, 1847. Born at Plaistow, N. H., Nov. 9, 1824. Spent seventeen years upon the farm with his father. Educated at country school and Lowell high school. Worked on iron in Lowell. Established the book and stationery business on Common St., Lawrence, 1847, from which he retired Nov., 1870, entering the crockery business in 1872. Married Mary Grafton Fenno, Dec. 3rd, 1850; has four sons. Attends Grace Episcopal Church. The establishment of the Lawrence Public Library is largely due to the exertions of Mr. Dow, and he is at present a member of its board of trustees.

epidemic, had its run and for a time carried everything before it, and during the war the Union sentiment and the Union party held full sway; but since the, war with occasionally an exceptional year, the contest for supremacy has been between the two great parties, and party lines definitely and rigorously drawn in Municipal as well as General elections. Now and then a "Citizens" movement has been inaugurated and carried through successfully; but a careful analysis of the interests which gave rise to the movement develops the fact that such movement generally originated in the party least hopeful of success at the polls, and while the great mass supporting it were honest and single minded, we feel constrained to say, that a few professional politicians found in such occasions an excellent opportunity for the development of their talents.

Perhaps the only election ever held in Lawrence where party politics did not directly or indirectly exert an influence was on the occasion of the first town meeting which was held Monday, April 26th, 1847, under a warrant issued by Dan Weed, Esq., directed to Charles S. Storrow. The charter had just gone into effect, the inhabitants were practically strangers to each other, and under these circumstances the best men were sought, regardless of party affiliation. Henry Flanders, a practising lawyer here, afterwards an eminent lawyer in Philadelphia, was elected moderator and E. W. Morse, town clerk; Daniel Saunders was elected treasurer, and the board of selectmen consisted of William Swan, Charles F. Abbott, Nathan Wells, James Stevens, and L. D. Brown; and for school committee men choice was made of James D. Herrick, Wm. D. Lamb and Dan Weed.

At a meeting held Friday, April 30th, in the same year, the town voted to raise four thousand five hundred dollars for town charges; twelve hundred dollars for the "repair and support of highways, town ways and bridges," and two thousand dollars for the support of schools for the year ensuing, and Bailey Bartlett was elected collector of taxes at a compensation of one per cent., which subsequently was made two per cent. The town also voted the "necessary sum or sums of money" to purchase two fire engines, and two thousand dollars for the purpose of building two school houses. The town being in a crysalis state, other town meetings as the needs of the town required were held during the year for the transaction of, to us, apparently unimportant business, but to them fraught with great responsibilities.

The March meeting of 1848 for the election of Town officers, witnessed the introduction of party lines in municipal affairs. Had the welfare of the nation depended upon the result, no greater emulation or resolution could have been displayed than was manifested.

William D. Joplin was elected Moderator on the first ballot, as was William Morse to the office of Town Clerk. For the other officers several ballots were taken and four attempts were made to elect selectmen before the board was filled, with the following named persons: David J. Clark, Charles F. Abbott, William D. Joplin, Levi Sprague and John M. Smith. No better success was had in the ballotings for the remaining officers. Somuch time was spent in this manner that an adjourned meeting was necessary for the transaction of the greater part of the business called for in the warrant. It having been voted to build a Town House its place of location became a mooted question. The suggestion to locate it on Jackson street, between Orchard and Garden streets was rejected. It was then decided to locate the building west of Appleton street and the proposition to locate it where it now is, was voted down, and a motion to build on the corner of Lawrence and Common streets was carried by ten majority, which vote was subsequently reconsidered and the present location decided upon, and under the direction of a special committee the building was erected, Charles Bean being the agent of the town. A motion to build a hall capable of seating three thousand people was carried, but the committee evidently did not closely fol-

EBENEZER B. CURRIER,

Real Estate Broker, 181 Essex St., Lawrence, Mass.; residence, 144 East Haverhill St. Born in Amesbury, Mass., May, 3, 1813. Went to Lowell in 1837, and worked at clerking a few years, subsequently entering the retail boot and shoe business on Merrimack St., manufacturing both for the wholesale and retail trade. Moved to Lawrence in 1847, and started the same business, in which he continued until 1852, the firm name being Footman & Currier. Representative to General Court in 1851, and it was through his efforts that the courts were removed to this city from Ipswich. Assessor the year the city charter was adopted and the year following. County commissioner for six years, beginning with 1855. Was inspector at State alms house in 1856–7. One of the inspectors at the house of correction in this city in 1865, and held the office six years. Has been justice of the peace since 1867.

low the instructions. Subsequent town meetings were as turbulent until the town became a city, and, generally speaking, the Whigs were in the ascendancy, although now and then a Democratic selectman or other town officer was chosen. The selectmen in 1849 were Levi Sprague, Charles F. Abbott and Isaac Fletcher. In 1850, Artemas Parker, Jr., William R. Page and William Gile. In 1851–52, William R. Page, Levi Sprague and Joseph Norris.

Our beautiful Common was the subject of much animated discussion in the town meetings held in 1848. The first recorded expression relating to it appears in the records of the meeting held April 17th, 1848, article 3d of the warrant being, "To see if the town will accept the land set apart by the Essex Company for a Common, and act thereon." Under this article a committee of five, consisting of S. H. Stevens, Ivan Stevens, A. Stevens, Jr., M. D. Ross and A. D. Blanchard, were appointed to confer with the Essex Company as to the conditions upon which they will deed the Common to the town." The committee reported the same day that "The Essex Company are not prepared to make any definite proposals of terms of deed." This report was accepted and the committee discharged.

A motion to instruct the selectmen "to accept a conveyance of the land laid out for a Common by the Essex Company," with such restrictions by the company as were not objectionable was amended by directing the appointment of a second committee of conference, which consisted of D. Saunders, Jr., J. D. Herrick, S. H. Stevens, Wm. A. Goodwin, and G. W. Sanborn, whose duty it was to ascertain the terms upon which the company would convey the land and the report of the committee was finally acted upon at a meeting held September 23d, the second article in the warrant being "to see if the town will accept the Common upon the conditions stated in the report of the committee appointed to confer with the Essex Company, etc." The vote being taken it was voted "not to accept the Common upon the conditions made by the Essex Company." At an adjourned meeting held October 7th, the voters had evidently received more light as to the intentions of the Essex Company for the records of that meeting are, "Charles Murch who voted with the majority moved a reconsideration of the vote passed September 23d, in relation to the acceptance of the Common," and the records continue after a vote to reconsider had been adopted, "Voted that the Common be accepted upon the conditions made by the Essex Company."

We have not space to spare for more than an outline of those early days. The town records of those times contain a mine of statistical wealth but valuable chiefly to the few who survive those days or the statistician. We have briefly touched upon the salient points in which the acts then done have directly affected to a greater or less extent the men and matters of the present day. They were earnest men, energetic men; they were and are the only kind of men that can found and build up a city. They had commenced a vast undertaking but they did not neglect small things. They were building for the future, and they "builded better than they knew." They were Democratic in its broadest and best sense, and believed in the government of the people by the people, and they zealously guarded every right. Their acceptance of the Common is an instance of this. They did not fail to appreciate the vast advantage of the gift of the Common by the Essex Company, but the tender was hampered by conditions which at first they deemed inimical, and they did not hesitate for a moment to decline its acceptance, and when the conditions were explained and fully understood, they with practical unanimity accepted what they had previously rejected. If one doubts their manliness and independence, they have but for a moment to consider that upon the Essex Company depended the material welfare of the town. The land, the power, all were vested in the great corporation, but the people neither truckled or bent the knee that "thrift might follow fawning," but sturdily kept their manhood, and their example has been felt all through the corporate life of the city.

DANIEL HARDY,

Residence, 268 Lowell Street. Has resided in Lawrence since May, 1846. Was born at Newburyport, Dec. 14, 1816. He was employed by the Eastern Railroad in Newburyport three years, and at Boston five years. He was connected with the Boston & Maine Railroad at Lawrence for twenty-eight years. Married to Ann P. Simonton of Portland, Oct. 27, 1844; has one child. Is connected with the Eliot Congregational church. Mr. Hardy served as school committeeman from 1856 to 1870 and from 1873 to 1876, making seventeen years. Was councilman in 1853, filled a vacancy in 1854, and was a member of the aldermanic board in 1866.

With the acceptance of the City Charter came, new duties, new responsibilities, and the clear cut outlines of individualism faded away, with here and there an exception, and men became merely the mass.

At the first city election in 1853, there were about 1000 names upon the voting list, and from the closeness with which the list was voted, (as shown by checks) it is inferred that nearly every one took an active interest in the proceedings. Of the voters upon the check list at that time about two hundred remain in the city to-day. Following is the list of those living here at present, as near as can be ascertained who voted at that election:

Armington, Pardon H.,
Allison, Samuel,
Andrews, W. H.,
Ambrose, Nathaniel,
Ames, Samuel,
Ayer, Perley,
Ames, Benjamin,
Armstrong, H. S.,
Blood, Albert,
Bailey, Heaton,
Barr, Thomas,
Bartlett, Bailey,
Battles, J. P.,
Belcher, Hiram,
Blanchard, A. D.,
Baldwin, Munroe,
Brewster, A. R.,
Briggs, Alanson,
Bunker, A. S.,
Berry, S. H.,
Bodwell, Asa M.,
Barker, Ebenezer,
Barnes, T. P.,
Beetle, John,
Blood, L. L.,
Brown, Asa N.,
Bryant, Amasa,
Burridge, J. Q. A.,
Burridge, William,
Butler, Frederick,
Buxton, Alonzo,
Cabot, George D.,
Chandler, H. P.,
Chadbourne, Benjamin F.,
Chapman, E. L.,
Clark, A. C.,
Clement, H. D.,
Conway, Thomas H.,
Chase, Charles,
Clark, A. P.,
Colby, J. S. M.,
Currier, E. B.,

Cheney, Bradford,
Churchill, Alfred,
Colby, William W.,
Currier, Alonzo K.,
Churchill, John,
Cate, T. J.,
Cahill, James,
Carter, Levi,
Clark, Albion G.,
Clifford, Thomas,
Closson, C. C.,
Crouse, John F.,
Caufy Edward,
Chandler, Abiel R.,
Carter, Levi H.,
Carter, Ebenezer,
Clark, James,
Colby, John,
Drake, N. P.,
Dow, John C.,
Drew, J. D.,
Durant, Adolphus,
Drew, F. C.,
Dana, David,
Damon, H. P.,
Doland, John J.,
Dolloff, E. B.,
Daly, Andrew,
Davis, S. M.,
Donovan, Timothy,
Durgin, H. J.,
Edwards, Franklin,
Fogg, James A.,
Fairfield, James M.,
Fletcher, Isaac,
Fay, A. M.,
Farnham, J. W.,
Flanders, Freeman,
Fuller, George A.,
Farrell, Henry,
Fisher, William,
Gallison, William B.,
Gardner, Isaac B.,
Gale, John,
Griffin, Benjamin,
Giles, A. W.,
Gleason, Justin,
Glidden, J. D.,
Goodrich, A. W.,
Gould, Samuel,
Holt, Nathan,
Hosmer, Abner,
Ham, H. S.,
Ham, F. B.,
Harmon, Nathan W.,
Hart, John,
Herrick, E. B.,
Hills, George W..
Hoadley, John C.,
Hutchinson, James S.,
Hatch, Seth,
Higgins, Amos,
Houghton, N. P.,
Hutchinson, John L.,

DAVID DANA,

Physician; office and residence, 35 Jackson St. Has been in Lawrence about 30 years. Born at Dedham, Mass., 1825. Was kept at school when young, and graduated from Harvard Medical College in 1847; spent one and one-half years in Boston public institutions as a physician. Married Dora Clark, in 1851; has two children. Attends Grace Episcopal Church. Has practiced medicine ever since coming to Lawrence. Was nearly two years in the War of the Rebellion, as surgeon of the 1st Mass. Heavy Artillery; taken prisoner at or near Centralville, in 1862, when from continued exposure to malarial poison in Virginia, he was sent home sick and obliged to resign. He has a pass given while prisoner by Gen. Lee, returning him to his regiment. Was the first city physician of Lawrence, and also the first physician appointed for the Jail and house of correction.

Ham, T. C.,
Howe, Merrill N.,
Hardy, Daniel,
Hamilton, O. B.,
Hart, Michael D.,
Herrick, J. D.,
James, Thomas,
Jordan, D. S.,
Joslyn, E. V.,
King, A. P. B.,
Knowles, Morris,
Knights, Samuel W.,
Kempton, J. G.,
Kendall, Thomas,
Kimball, W. A.,
Knox, Otis,
Kelley, Daniel H.,
Lamb, William D.,
Low, T. B.,
Lyford, W. S.,
Littlefield, George,
Ladd, Luther,
Lewis, Rodney, A.,
Lindsay, Thomas L.,
Leeman, Wellington,
Massey, Joseph,
Mallard, Lauren,
Merriam, J. F.,
Merriam, Thatcher,
McAllister, William,
Miles, James,
Morrissey, John,
Melvin, N. P. H.,
Moore, William H.,
Morrison, Abiel,
Murphy, Patrick,
McClure, William T.,
McCarty, John,
Merrill, Charles R.,
Minehan, Edward,
Moore, Larkin,
Morse, D. A.,
Noyes, Henry,
Noyes, B. C.,
Ordway, Aaron,
Osgood, Timothy,
O'Reilley, Thomas,
Porter, David T.,
Poulson, Alexander,
Parsons, Thomas A.,
Page, Edward,
Pearl, Oliver,
Perkins, J. S.,
Pillsbury. C. K.,
Payson, Carleton,
Perkins, A. J.,
Phelps, Augustus,
Phillips, H. H.,
Pillsbury, Joshua,
Pingree, William E.,
Poor, Edward P.,
Pedrick, William R.,
Pearsons, A. G.,
Perkins, Moses,

Plummer, H.,
Poor, Samuel,
Poor, George,
Proctor, Moses,
Putnam, Albert M.,
Reed, Rufus,
Rollins, John R.,
Robinson, D. F.,
Rossiter, Ambrose,
Richardson, Eli,
Richardson, D. C.,
Robinson, Gilman B.,
Rogers, Thomas C.,
Spalding, Wm. R.,
Stratton, Lewis,
Sullivan, William,
Sutcliffe, Phillip,
Saunders, Daniel,
Scott, Thomas,
Smith, Charles,
Sweeney, Patrick,
Sanborn, George,
Sargent, L. D.,
Sargent, Moses.,
Simmons, S. P.,
Stannard, James H.,
Stearns, A. W.,
Stoddard, Leonard,
Stoddard, R. S.,
Stearns, Samuel,
Stowell, Joseph,
Smith, Charles M.,
Salisbury, Geo. W.,
Sargent, Edwin,
Shattuck, Joseph,
Smith, John,
Smith, William B.,
Stevens, Abiel,
Stevens, Warren,
Stevens, Ivan,
Stoddard, Alphonso,
Stokes, Joel,
Stone, Thomas,
Stone, John,
Sibley, Kneeland,
Tewksbury, Isaac,
True, Ira,
Tims, Henry,
Trull, Elijah,
Valpey, D. S. A.,
Varnum, L. N.,
Wadleigh, J. C.,
Webster, D. B.,
Whitney, H. M.,
Wright, W. H. P.,
Wiley, W. A.,
Wallace, S. Y.,
Webster, Abel,
Wells, Nathan,
White, N. G.,
Wilson, Allen,
Wood, James M.,
Wright, A. S.,
Wood, Emerson,

SAMUEL M. DAVIS,

Real Estate Broker. Office at North Depot; residence, 36 Winter St. Born at Parsonsfield, Me., Feb. 24, 1820. Came to Lawrence in 1847. Was engineer on the Boston & Maine Railroad, running the first locomotive into Lawrence over the railroad bridge, and also ran the first passenger train on the Manchester & Lawrence Railroad. Member of the common council in 1861, and of the board of alderman in 1867, 1868, 1869. Is a member of the board of health for the present year. Has been a justice of the peace since 1870. Mr. Davis has always taken an active part in municipal matters. Married Almedia C. Small of Limington, Me., in 1852; has three children. Attends the Baptist church.

Withington, Henry,
Wade, A. M.,
Williams, Cyrus,
Walker, A. J.,
Warren, Albert,
Webster, T. K.,
Weeks, Benjamin,
Wingate, Moses,
Waterhouse, Gideon W.,
Yeaton, Philip,
Yates, Stephen D.

In the month of March, 1853, the legal voters were called together to vote on the acceptance of the City Charter. The result was yeas, 659; nays, 143.

The election for Mayor was April 18th, when there were two ballots taken, and a third and final one May 7th, with the following result: Charles S. Storrow had 577; Dana Sargent, 484; scattering, 21.

At this election there was considerable interest felt. While many thought that to Mr. Storrow, the efficient agent of the Essex Company, who from the commencement of the new settlement had felt the deepest interest in everything relating to the material prosperity of the new enterprise, the compliment of the position of first Mayor properly belonged. Others feared that there was danger of corporation influence having too complete predominance, and claimed that the interests of the corporations and those of the city were diverse and conflicting, but the result showed that such fear was without cause, for a more acceptable Chief Magistrate the city has never enjoyed. Mr. Storrow was elected on the third ballot as the candidate of the Whig party. Mr. Sargent that of the Democratic.

* 1854. The second election was a spirited one, the third and last ballot resulting as follows: Enoch Bartlett received 651 votes, Geo. W. Benson, 529, James D. Herrick, 67, scattering, 12. Mr. Bartlett, candidate of the Democratic party, a young lawyer of considerable promise, was elected over Mr. Benson, the Whig candidate, also a promising lawyer universally esteemed, who the previous year had acted as City Clerk, and Mr. Herrick was the candidate of the Free

* The election was held the December previous.

Soil party, which was then feebly working its way up with little prospect of ever assuming the power and strength and majesty of the great Republican party of United States. Mr. Bartlett unfortunately soon after his election had the misfortune to experience loss of health, and shortly after the end of his official term, went home to New Hampshire, his native State, to die.

During this year commenced the great Know Nothing uprising, and the worry and excitement attendant upon the popular demonstrations, at times threatening the peace of the community, taxed the waning energies of our Mayor to an extent beyond their capacity.

1855. This year the Know Nothings swept the city, Albert Warren Know Nothing candidate receiving 1037 votes, E. F. Bean, Democrat, 81, N. W. Harmon, Whig, 82, scattering, 7. There was no occasion for three ballots as heretofore, the election being "like the handle to a jug, all on one side." The Whig and Democratic parties having respectively dwindled down to a very few on either side who had little fear of the Pope of Rome making America his immediate headquarters. The sweep in Lawrence, however, was no more general than throughout the State, and Messrs. Harmon and Bean had no more cause to feel surprised or chagrined at their feeble following, than the Whig and Democratic candidates for public support had elsewhere throughout the Commonwealth.

1856. This year the vote stood, Albert Warren, 758 votes: John R. Rollins, 386. The election was a repetition of the year before, the Democrats making no nomination, and Mr. Rollins consequently received the support of all persons not in affiliation with the dominant party, which as yet showed no symptoms of dissolution, although in fact so near its end.

1857. This year John R. Rollins received 801 votes, Thomas Wright, 570, scattering, 6. Politics were not strictly defined. The Republican party had not yet assumed form and proportion. Both

JAMES STUART BARRIE,

Grocer, 122 Essex St.; residence, 63 High St. Has been in Lawrence twenty-nine years. Born in Stirlingshire, Scotland, 1837. Worked in the factories in his boyhood; learned the trade of wool-sorting, at which he worked for seventeen years, using his evenings for self-education. Married Mary Adelaide Morrill of Amesbury in 1860; has two children. Attends the Garden St. Episcopal Methodist church. Mr. Barrie is an earnest worker in the labor interest, a member of the Labor Reform State Central Committee, and has been closely connected with all temperance movements, having been a candidate for the legislature on the prohibition ticket in 1873, since which he has affiliated with the republican party, holding various offices. Was president of the common council in 1877, and is at present president of the board of health.

Messrs. Rollins and Wright were Whigs, and supporters of Gen. Winfield Scott in the Presidential election of this year, although many Whigs on this occasion refrained from voting at all, and not a few voted for his opponent, Gen. Pierce. The city at this time was strongly anti-democratic, and an outright Democratic nominee would have shown but a feeble following. Mr. Rollins was the nominee of the Whig party and Mr. Wright received the support of the disaffected, whatever their nation, kind or condition.

1858. John R. Rollins had 762 votes, N. G. White, 538, Nathaniel G. White, 76, scattering, 11. This was almost a repetition of the preceding year, both Messrs. Rollins and White were members of the Whig party. Mr. Rollins being re-nominated by his party as before, and Mr. White receiving the support of the Democratic party and disaffected generally.

1859. This was probably the most spirited municipal contest our city ever witnessed. Henry K. Oliver, the Republican nominee, received 886 votes, Daniel Saunders, Jr., 589, scattering, 5.

Republicanism had assumed somewhat fixed proportions and dimensions, and Gen. Oliver was the nominee of that party, and Mr. Saunders of the Democratic, but politics were disregarded to quite a general extent. Mr. Saunders had the support of some of the most active Republicans, and Gen. Oliver the support of influential Democratic Catholics and their followers. Feeling run high, but the Irish support being finally secured in favor of the latter, he was elected by quite a decided majority.

1860. This year the political pot was turned over. Daniel Saunders, Jr., the Democratic nominee having 810 votes, and John R. Rollins, the Republican, having 646. Mr. Rollins, yielding to the solicitation of his party made the dangerous experiment of running for a third time. During the first month of this year occurred the terrible disaster of the fall of the Pemberton Mill, thus throwing upon the new Mayor a care, responsibility and duty such as no previous one had been called to assume.

1861. This year James K. Barker was the Republican candidate, and Benjamin F. Watson the Democratic, and the actual standing of the two respective parties at that time can be fairly judged by the result of this election. Mr. Barker had 967 votes, Mr. Watson, 567, scattering, 3. Mr. Watson was an active, energetic politician, prominent and popular in his party, and a lawyer of first rate standing, with personal friends in abundance in all quarters of the city. He conducted the campaign personally and infused into his followers his own individual energy, spirit and dash, but things looked ominous abroad. There was an angry spirit in the South,—Lincoln was just elected President of the United States, and men stuck rigidly to their party regardless of private personal feeling. This was the first year of the war and on that account is memorable.

1862. During the interim since last election, the Rebellion had broken out and with it came new responsibilities, new issues. The Republican party had become strongly cemented together, Mr. Wright was the popular war candidate, and in fact the better classes mostly rallied to his support. The vote stood, W. H. P. Wright, 805, N. G. White, 506, James K. Barker, 87.

1863. The same issues upon which the previous campaign was fought entered into this issue. The vote was, W. H. P. Wright, 719, N. P. H. Melvin, 474, Nathaniel H. P. Melvin, 158.

1864. This year the Republicans entered the campaign with Dr. A. J. French as standard bearer, while the opposition of all classes centered their strength upon John Beetle as a citizens' candidate. The vote was, A. J. French, 720, John Beetle, 615.

1865. The war party were early in the field for this campaign, and by selecting Mr. Bonney as candidate the opposition was feeble. The vote was, Milton Bonney, 762, N. Chapman, 270.

EUGENE S. YATES,

Physician and Surgeon, at 307 Essex St.; residence, 28 Summer St. Has resided in Lawrence since 1847. Was born at Locke's Mills, Me., Oct. 22, 1845. Educated at the public schools of the city, graduating from the high school in class of '64. Enlisted May 10, 1864 in Capt. Hamilton's Company, 8th Unattached, for three months; stationed at Galloupe's Island, Boston Harbor; mustered out Aug. 11, 1864. Was letter-carrier at Lawrence Post Office for the remainder of the year. Re-enlisted Jan. 2, 1865 in Co. D, Frontier Cavalry, stationed at Ogdensburg, N. Y.; mustered out June 30, 1865. Worked for Dr. Aaron Ordway, as apothecary clerk, from Aug. 9, 1865 to Nov. 9, 1869, when he entered Harvard Medical College, graduating at Bellevue Hospital Medical College, New York City, class of '72; has practiced in this city since then. Married Miss Cora G. Elliott of Fisherville, N. H., May 6, 1872. Attends the First Baptist church. City Physician for 1878, and also a member of Lawrence Board of Health.

1866. The "boys" had come marching home before this municipal election. In the fall of 1865 when the election came off there was considerable dissatisfaction in municipal affairs, and many of the prominent so called leaders decided to support N. G. White upon a citizens' ticket. Mr. White refused to have his name used without some sort of assurance that such a step was desirable on the part of a large number of influential citizens. His friends therefore circulated petitions requesting him to allow his name to be used. These were signed by over 800 voters, but for some cause the movement fell into disrepute, the poorer classes thinking it a movement in favor of the capitalist, and Pardon Armington was taken up as "Sam's" candidate, and with a short but vigorous campaign he was elected by a small majority. The year 1866 will be remembered as the most wasteful and improvident city government ever organized. The vote was, Pardon Armington, 894. N. G. White, 828.

1867. The Republican party and its manipulators had fallen into disrepute and the Democrats carried the city by a small majority. N. P. H. Melvin had 959, L. A. Bishop, 831.

1868. Mr. Melvin proving himself a most efficient public servant was elected without any determined opposition. N. P. H. Melvin had 1406 votes, Fred Butler, 668.

1869. By Mr. Melvin's square and straightforward action he had displeased many party adherents and the Republicans in the mean time having increased so that with a fair degree of unity they could succeed, rallied on Major Frank Davis as their candidate. The contest was lively and a full vote was polled. Frank Davis was elected, having 1551 votes, against 1396 for N. P. H. Melvin.

1870. Mr. Melvin was again the standard bearer of the Democratic party, and his known ability gave him a goodly number of votes outside his party, securing his election. The vote stood, N. P. H. Melvin, 1518, John B. Atkinson, 1363.

Since that time the causes which have transpired to produce the results are quite familiar to most of the residents of to-day. A recapitulation simply of the vote is therefore only appended for each municipal year.

1871. S. B. W. Davis, 1665, John J. Doland, 1522.

1872. S. B. W. Davis, 1726, John J. Doland, 1604, Daniel Hardy, 55.

1873. John K. Tarbox, 1959, S. B. W. Davis, 1685.

1874. John K. Tarbox, 2211, scattering, 24.

1875. R. H. Tewksbury, 2396, N. P. H. Melvin, 1555.

1876. Edmund R. Hayden, 2162, Wm. S. Knox, 1843.

1877. Caleb Saunders, 2283, A. A. Currier, 2010.

1878. James R. Simpson, 2365, Caleb Saunders, 1795.

The following tables will show the comparative increase in municipal wealth :

	Ratable Polls.	*Valuation.*
1847,	23	$1,719,204
1848,	497	3,814,426
1849,	1,321	5,730,710
1850,	2,318	5,902,741
1851,	2,249	6,407,926
1852,	2,542	6,374,355
1853,	2,514	6,937,160
1854,	3,096	8,842,915
1855,	3,366	9,954,041
1856,	3,689	10,483,725
1857,	3,525	10,227,310
1858,	3,688	10,249,009
1859,	2,932	10,022,947
1860,	3,057	10,584,023
1861,	3,609	10,269,615
1862,	3,906	10,777,920

EDWARD CAUFY,

Station Agent at Boston & Maine north depot. Residence, 10 Morton St. Was born in St. Albans, Me., July 26th, 1831. Left home at the age of 16, and worked at lumbering in his native state till 1849, when he came to Lawrence and worked for the Essex Co. two years. Entered the employ of the B. & M. Railroad in 1851, as conductor of shifting trains. Enlisted in Co. I, 6th Reg't, April 16, 1861, and was with the regiment in its "march through Baltimore." Enlisted in the 26th Regiment the same year, and was commissioned 1st lieutenant of Co. F, 1862. Four months after was commissioned captain of Co. B, and held that position until the close of the war. In 1873 was promoted to station agent by the Boston & Maine Company.

	Ratable Polls.	Valuation.
1863,	3,378	10,937,450
1864,	3,282	11,074,430
1865,	3,692	12,783,273
1866,	4,147	13,748,285
1867,	5,250	14,684,000
1868,	5,714	15,569,500
1869,	5,960	16,647,000
1870,	6,316	17,912,500
1871,	6,006	18,552,000
1872,	6,625	20,763,663
1873,	7,000	21,687,732
1874.	7,577	22,918,775
1875,	7,728	24,117,475
1876,	8,120	23,902,599
1877,	8,026	23,902,537
1878,	8,540	23,714,017

X.

PUBLIC SCHOOLS.

In 1845, when the Essex Company commenced operations within the limits of the territory which now constitutes Lawrence, the portion north of the Merrimack River was a part of Methuen, and the portion south of the river was a part of Andover. There were in the territory three one-story schoolhouses, looking like those which were then to be seen in the sparsely populated districts of Massachusetts, one of the two in the Methuen portion giving no perceptible evidence that it had ever been painted; the other showing that it had once been painted red, while the one on the south side still retained a yellowish tinge. Our fathers were nobly desirous that every child should be taught the rudiments of education, and they provided schools for them, but they seemed to think little of making the schoolhouse comfortable or attractive. In these houses, one upon Tower Hill, the second at the intersection of what are now Prospect and East Haverhill Streets, and the third on the south side, near the intersection of the Lowell road and the Turnpike, there were summer and winter schools of a few weeks' duration.

In the year 1846, the Essex Company erected a schoolhouse between Haverhill and Tremont Streets, where a school was opened under the direction of the Methuen School Committee, on the 7th of November, by Nathaniel Ambrose as teacher. He commenced with

GILBERT EDWIN HOOD.

Was born in Chelsea, Vt., November 21st, 1824; lived upon his father's farm until he was 21 years old. Graduated at Dartmouth College in 1851. Taught school before, during and after his college course. Married Frances E. Herrick of Danvers, Mass., in 1852. Was admitted to the Bar in Boston in 1855. Commenced the practice of law in Lawrence in 1859, and has resided here ever since. Has held the positions of Associate Justice of Lawrence Police Court, City Solicitor, Register of Deeds, Superintendent of Schools, for twelve years, and is at present Treasurer of the Broadway Savings Bank.

twenty-five scholars, but before the expiration of its first year it numbered one hundred and fifty scholars.

April 17th, 1847, the act of incorporation of the Town of Lawrence was signed by the Governor, and April 26th there was a town meeting for the choice of officers. The whole number of votes thrown was 164. A School Committee of three were chosen,—James D. Herrick, Dan Weed, and Wm. D. Lamb, M. D., two of whom are still residents of our city. At their second meeting it was voted that one male teacher and five female teachers be employed, Mr. Ambrose as male teacher in the Essex Company's house, Miss Robinson for the Durant District, Miss Ford for the Tower Hill District, Miss Brown and Miss Abbott for the Free Will Baptist Vestry, and Miss Odell on the south side of the river.

During this year, a story and a half schoolhouse was built on Jackson street, where the Unitarian church now stands, and a similar one upon the Lowell road on the south side of the river.

At the annual town meeting held March 1848, a school committee of five were chosen, consisting of J. D. Herrick, of the previous committee, and Nathan W. Harmon, Henry F. Harrington, Lyman Whiting, and George Packard, two of whom are still residents of the city. The committee, early in the year, and after consultation with Hon. Horace Mann and other distinguished educators, adopted the system of schools, which with our small territorial area, was deemed the best for us, consisting of primary, intermediate or middle schools, scattered over the territory of the town; one grammar school upon the North Side of the river in some central position, one Grammar School upon the South Side, and one High School for the whole town. At the first meeting of the Committee, held March 13th, a sub-committee was appointed to confer with the town's finance committee upon the absolute necessity of additional room for four hundred scholars, and the obligation of the town by statute to provide a High

School. The finance committee reported in favor of an appropriation of $12,500 for the erection of an edifice of the capacity demanded.

April 3d, a male teacher was placed over the Grammar School on South Side. April 13th, Geo. A. Walton was elected master of the Grammar School on the north side of the river, and which was then kept in the Jackson street house. Mr. Walton's connection with that school was commenced April 17th, 1848, and was continued without interruption until the summer of 1864; and during these more than sixteen years he was the earnest, devoted teacher, under whose management the school was, what one of our reports said of it,—an admirably ordered, well instructed and happy Grammar School.

At the School Committee meeting held November 14th, 1848, Rev. Mr. Harrington reported the gift of school apparatus from Gen. H. K. Oliver, and the following vote was passed: "That as General Oliver, had tendered to the committee the gift of a valuable philosophical and astronomical apparatus for the use of the High School of this town, his generous offer be gratefully accepted, and the chairman be authorized to receive the same agreeably to the wishes of the donor." At the meeting of the committee held November 21st, it was voted "That the upper rooms of the new School House be devoted to the use of the Grammar School, and the front room of the lower story be devoted to the use of the High School."

1849, January 17, Mr. Thomas W. T. Curtis was examined, and elected teacher of the High School.

The time for dedicating the new School House on Haverhill Street, was fixed for January 30th, and at a meeting of the school committee the evening previous, it was voted, "To proceed to the choice of a name for the new School House." Voted, "That the School to be hereafter kept in the School House on Haverhill Street, in town of Lawrence, shall bear the name of the Oliver School, and

JOHN F. COGSWELL,

Cogswell & Co.'s Express, office, 5 Lawrence Street; residence, 276 Haverhill St. Born at Dover, N. H., March, 1835. Educated at Phillips Academy, Andover. Came to Lawrence in 1853. He was employed at the Pacific Mills four years, and by the Boston & Maine Co. two years. Entered the express business in 1859, and has continued in it since that time. Attends Grace Episcopal church. Was a member of common council in 1862-63, and is at present one of the trustees of the city library; also a trustee of the Broadway Savings Bank. Married Esther M. Merrill in 1860; has two children.

that this name shall be publicly announced by the chairman of the school committee in the words of the above vote."

January 31st, the Committee met at the Oliver School House, and after examination, seventeen were admitted to the High School. September 4th, of that same year, another examination of candidates took place, but none were admitted.

The High School continued under the sole charge of Mr. Curtis, with about twenty scholars, until that number was increased by the admission of twenty-two scholars, September 2d, 1850, seven only without qualification. October 24th Miss Sarah B. Hooker was elected assistant teacher, whose subsequent course fully sustained the high expectations formed from her appearance and examination.

During the municipal year ending March 1st, 1850, the Amesbury Street School House, the Newbury Street School House, and the School House on Tower Hill, which was called the Pine Grove School House, were built. During the year ending March, 1851, a better School House was built on the South Side of the river, opposite the residence of M. C. Andrews, and also the Cross Street House, and a one-story, and what was considered a temporary house on Oak Street, in the rear of the Oliver School House. A plan was also submitted by the School Committee for the enlargement of the Oliver School House, by building a transverse section, three stories in height, furnishing in the upper story a large and commodious hall, and in the second and first stories, eight rooms. At the close of the fourth municipal year there were seventeen distinct schools under the care of twenty-five teachers, and having an attendance of 1470 scholars.

From the first, the town met with prompt liberality every reasonable demand made by the School Committee, but those demands could not be properly anticipated. Neither the town authorities nor the School Committee had data by which they could calculate with certainty the School accommodations that would be required in any specified time. The School report for the year ending March, 1850, says: "When the Oliver School House was planned, no idea of a Grammar School was associated with the premises, as it was supposed that the Jackson Street House would accommodate the Grammar School on this side of the river, for an indefinite period. But before the walls were up it was found necessary entirely to alter the plan, and the Grammar School was placed in its upper story, with seats for 184 scholars." And although the house was dedicated January 30th, 1849, the report further states, the accommodations it furnishes have long been insufficient. In the report of the next year, from March 31, 1850 to March 31, 1851, when advocating the necessary enlargement of the building, the committee said: "It is a matter of profound thanksgiving on our part, in view of our official responsibility, that we are not answerable for the extraordinary increase of the children of this town." Our predecessors recommended that a new house should be built for the middle and primary schools now kept in the Oliver House, and the rooms they had occupied be devoted to the Grammar School, adding: This arrangement will answer, it is hoped for several years. Several years? It was not several months,—indeed, the arrangement had not been carried into effect before the increase of scholars was such as to leave everything worse off than before. One hundred and twenty-five children, the report farther says "are now waiting for room in the Oliver School House." With good reason, therefore, the committee urged the addition of the large transverse section.

Since that addition was made there has never been the uncomfortable pressure of necessity, so very difficult to provide for, that for so many years harrassed the Committee.

In the year ending March, 1852, the Unitarian Vestry, which was on Jackson Street, and had been for some years occupied as a School House, was purchased and removed to the intersection of Newbury and Elm Streets, and has been and is known as the Elm Street School House.

ALBERT DAVID SWAN,

Fire Insurance Agent. Office at No. 7 Lawrence Street; residence, corner of Andover St. and Winthrop Ave. Has been in Lawrence since 1848, excepting from 1861 to 1866. Born in Tewksbury, Middlesex Co., Mass., May 10, 1845. Attended the Oliver Grammar and Lawrence High School; graduated at Comer's Commercial College, Boston. Married Helen Eliza Churchill, May 10th, 1866; has no children. Unitarian in belief. Commenced as clerk in the private banking house of Hallgarten & Herzfield, New York City; was afterwards gold paying teller and also attorney for the firm in the New York Stock Board. Started in company with his father, under the firm name of D. S. Swan & Son, in 1866, in the Fire Insurance Agency business, which he has continued to the present. The senior member of the firm died in 1874. Mr. Swan was paymaster of the 2nd Bat. Mass. Light Art., and is now mustering officer and paymaster of the 1st Bat. Light Art. A director of Bay State National Bank.

In the year 1854, the Hampshire Street School House, called in the late School Reports, the Pine Street House, and the Franklin Street School House were built.

In the year 1856, the small one-story School House, which, at the commencement of Lawrence was found at what is now the junction of Prospect and East Haverhill Streets, and which had been several times repaired and improved, gave place to a two story School House of a similar plan with the other wooden School Houses in the city, and the one story house on Oak Street was converted into a two story house, furnishing four rooms for one middle, and three graded primary schools, and this same year an addition of a second room for the primary school was made in the Amesbury Street house.

In 1860, the Grammar School House on the South Side was moved to the spot which it now occupies, and a large addition made to it, so that for a time the primary, middle and grammar schools of that part of the town were accommodated in that one building.

In 1861, a two story School House of wood was built at the corner of Lowell and Margin Streets, at the foot of Tower Hill, and the Pine Grove house was removed from the summit to the southern base of the hill for the accommodation of the primary school children between the hill and the river.

In 1862, the School House at the intersection of Methuen and Newbury Streets was built, the only addition made to the School Houses that year.

The School Committee, when pressed above measure for room to furnish sittings to the children clamoring for admission to the schools, have resorted to the religious societies for their lecture rooms and vestries, and oftentimes with no little inconvenience to themselves, those societies have allowed their use. Schools have been kept in the Free Will Baptist, the First Baptist, the Lawrence Street Congregational, the Central Congregational, the Unitarian and the Presbyterian societies.

In May, 1866, the following preamble and resolution were adopted by the School Committee.

Whereas, The present accommodations of the Oliver Grammar School building are insufficient to meet the wants of the school, and whereas the room now occupied by the Oliver High School is much needed for the Oliver Grammar School, therefore

Resolved, That this Board would respectfully recommend that the City Council take measures to secure a new building for the Oliver High School, at as early a day as is practicable."

In the year 1865, under Hon. Milton Bonney as Mayor, the City Government, in anticipation of this necessity, with prudent foresight, secured suitable grounds for the erection of such a building, and the City Government of 1866, under Hon. Pardon Armington as Mayor, obtained plans, contracted for and commenced the erection of such a building as shall meet the present and prospective wants of the school.

In the early part of the year 1867, anticipating the removal of the High School to the house designed for its use, alterations were made in the Oliver Grammar School House for the better accommodation of its pupils. As a commodious hall was to be provided in the High School building, which could be used by the Grammar School at its annual exhibitions, the hall of the Grammar School building was divided into three rooms, one, a large room capable of seating half of the school for general exercises in music, etc., and two other rooms of the same size as in other parts of the building for the use of a division of the school or a section of a division. In the summer vacation, the front portion of the building was raised one story so as to bring it to the same elevation with the transverse portion, and there was built a spacious and most convenient stairway, with ample clothes rooms for the scholars of each school room. There are now in the Oliver School House sixteen rooms occupied by classes, and the large room, which can seat comfortably four hundred children.

ALBERT FERNANDO COLBURN,

Stationer and Newsdealer, (Colburn Bros.) 281 Essex St.; residence, 23 Orchard St. Has been in Lawrence twenty-nine years. Born in Dracut, near Lowell, October 8, 1834. Attended the grammar school under the principalship of George A. Walton, afterwards entering the employ of Bean & Whittier, furniture dealers, and continuing in that business until the firm of Colburn Bro's was formed in 1873. For a number of years Mr. Colburn took an active part in politics, and was a member of the city council from Ward I, in 1867. He was also a member of the fire department for a number of years, prior to the advent of steamers, and was captain of Niagara Engine Co., No. 2, at the time of the disbanding of the hand engine companies. He is at present an active member of numerous secret societies, and is also a member of the Universalist society.

The building will allow of eight hundred and forty scholars, and is, in the arrangement of its rooms, its spacious and safe stairways, its commodious clothes rooms, indeed in all of its interior arrangements, a house which is not equalled, certainly not excelled, by any in the State.

From this general review of our schools, we now speak particularly of the High School.

In 1848, in the second year of the municipal organization, measures were adopted for the establishment of a High School. In November of that year, Gen. Oliver made a donation of valuable philosophical and astronomical apparatus for its use.

January 17th, 1849, Mr. Thomes T. Curtis was elected teacher of the High School, and January 31st, seventeen were admitted to membership in the school.

September 2d, 1850, twenty-two scholars were admitted, and October 24th Miss Sarah B. Hooker was elected assistant.

July, 1857, Mr. Curtis resigned the office of Principal, much to the regret of the committee, and for the remaining four weeks of the term Rev. Henry F. Harrington kindly officiated in his place.

September, 1851, Mr. C. J. Pennel, whom the committee had elected to the office of Principal, entered upon his duties, with Miss Hooker as assistant.

January 21st, 1852, Miss Hooker resigned her position, a step, as the school report says, deeply lamented by the committee and the school, with the parents of the scholars, and the many who had witnessed her peculiar aptness in teaching. The committee very fortunately obtained the temporary services of Miss Jane S. Gerrish, who was very soon elected as assistant, an office which she retained 21 years with the highest credit to herself, and to the entire satisfaction of successive committees.

In July, 1853, Mr. Pennel, to the regret of the committee, resigned the Principalship of the school, to take a professorship in Antioch

College, Ohio, and Mr. Samuel J. Pike, then a tutor in Bowdoin College, Maine, was elected to the position, and entered upon his duties in September.

A louder call being made to Mr. Pike from the school committee of Somerville, he resigned his position soon after the commencement of the Fall term of 1856. His three years of service were faithfully and acceptably passed.

In June, 1856, Miss Harriet C. Hovey was elected as second assistant, and in this same month Gen. Oliver generously donated to the school department, for the benefit of the High School, a fine engraving of the Landing of the Pilgrims, and also one of the Battle of Bunker Hill, together with busts of Cicero, Demosthenes, Socrates, Plato, Franklin and Washington, and statuettes of Galileo, Bowditch, Dante, Goethe, Schiller, Tasso, Ariosto and Petrarch. They have adorned the walls of the High School room in the Oliver School House, and at the donor's request they have been transferred to the school room of the new building.

For a few months after the withdrawal of Mr. Pike, the position of Principal was filled by Mr. Wm. H. Farrar, and May 2d, 1857, Mr. William J. Rolfe was elected to the office. After a service of four and a half years, on August 27th, 1861, he tendered his resignation, which was reluctantly accepted by the committee, with the following resolution:

Resolved, That the School Committee of Lawrence hereby express their just appreciation of the diligence and fidelity of Mr. Rolfe, during his connection with the Oliver High School as Principal, of his mode of instruction, well adapted to awaken a spirit of inquiry and research, and of the high standard to which his labors have contributed so largely to raise the school; and that we hereby commend him to others as a thorough and critical scholar and an excellent instructor.

PRESCOTT GROSVENOR PILLSBURY,

Cashier of Lawrence National Bank, Brechin Block, corner of Broadway and Essex St. Has been in Lawrence ten years. Was born in Newburyport, Mass., June 13, 1846. He removed in early youth to Haverhill and was educated in the public schools of that city. Vestryman at Grace Episcopal church. Spent one year in the counting room of Gooding & Johnson, Haverhill; was for four years clerk and teller in the First National Bank in Haverhill. Came to Lawrence in 1868, entering the Bay State National Bank, in which he served four years as teller; was appointed cashier of the Lawrence National Bank, upon its organization in 1872; is one of the trustees of the Broadway Savings Bank. Appointed justice of the peace by Gov. Washburne in 1873. Mr. Pillsbury was a member of the common council from Ward III, for the years 1875–6.

For three months succeeding Mr. Rolfe's resignation, the committee were enabled to secure the services of Mr. Thomas G. Valpey, a highly competent instructor in another institution then in vacation. December 1st, 1861, Mr. Henry L. Boltwood, who had been elected to the office of Principal, entered upon his duties.

May 8th, 1863, Miss Hovey, after seven years cheerful and faithful labor, resigned the situation of assistant, which was filled by the election of Miss Marcia Packard. In June of that year Mr. Boltwood resigned his situation, which was temporarily filled by Mr. I. H. Ward from the Theological school at Andover.

At a meeting of the committee, held August 5th, 1863, Mr. Albert C. Perkins was elected Principal, and he entered upon his duties September 7th.

No change occurred in principal till the year 1873, when Albert C. Perkins tendered his resignation to accept the position of principal of Phillips Exeter Academy. During his ten years' service in the High School he did much to raise its standard and was in every respect a most thorough disciplinarian. The same year Miss Packard and Miss Gerrish resigned. Mr. Charles T. Lazelle succeeded as principal and Miss Alice Birtwell and Miss Alice Carter as assistants. In 1872 Mr. Herbert S. Rice was employed as Teacher of Drawing, a position which he filled acceptably for nearly five years.

In 1875 Mr. Horace E. Bartlett was called to the principalship—a position he now occupies. The teachers of the High School the present year are Horace E. Bartlett, Parker P. Simmons, Mary A. Newell, Emily G. Wetherbee, Alice Birtwell, Ada Leah, Katharine A. O'Keeffe.

The masters of the Oliver School following Mr. Walton were James H. Eaton, John L. Brewster, James Barrell, and the present master, Park S. Warren.

The South Lawrence male teachers have been Mr. Ayer in 1848,

Mr. Tenney, J. B. Fairfield, W. Fisk Gile, John Orne, J. Henry Root, J. K. Cole, and the present Grammar master, Edward P. Shute. Ayer and Tenney taught in the School House on the Lowell road. Mr. Fairfield taught from January 1851 till some time in 1858 in a building that stood where Mr. A. D. Swan's residence now stands. W. Fisk Gile taught in the same place, and also Mr. Orne. The School was then transferred to where the Saunders School now is. Mr. Root taught in the new building. Mr. Cole began there and went to the present Packard School building when it was completed. Mr. Cole taught longer than any other male teacher there.

In 1869 the Cross Street School House was repaired and enlarged, and a new school house built at the corner of Woodland and Pleasant streets. In 1870 the Oak Street house was completed. In 1872 the brick School House, dedicated as the Packard School was completed. In 1873 the Woodland Street School House was enlarged to three times its former capacity, and a new brick School House containing four large rooms built on East Elm Street, and when dedicated the following season was named the Harrington School. In 1875 the Franklin Street School House was enlarged, a new house built on Hancock Street, and the substantial brick house on Washington Street commenced, which was completed the following year.

In 1876 a new building was erected in Ward Six, corner of Union and Andover Streets, and in 1877 the Franklin Street School House was enlarged to admit of four Schools.

The School Superintendents of Lawrence have been: John A. Goodwin from 1853 to 1854; Henry F. Harrington, 1854–55; Geo. Packard, 1855–56 ;, and 1859–61; A. Williams, 1856–7; Henry K. Oliver, 1857–9; Joseph L. Partridge, 1861–64; John R. Rollins, January to June in the year 1864; Gilbert E. Hood, June, 1864, to January, 1877; Harrison Hume began January 1, 1877, and is still in office.

The following table will show the comparative increase of School children since the beginning of the city:

Year	Number	Year	Number
1845,	40	1862,	3,310
1847,	800	1863,	3,384
1848,	900	1864,	3,495
1849,	1,527	1865,	3,613
1850,	1,470	1866,	4,026
1851,	1,709	1867,	4,432
1852,	1,650	1868,	4,359
1853,	1,869	1869,	4,665
1854,	2,167	1870,	4,846
1855,	2,518	1871,	4,856
1856,	2,792	1872,	4,847
1857,	3,022	1873,	5,141
1858,	2,610	1874,	5,385
1859,	2,702	1875,	5,648
1860,	3,171	1876,	5,634
1861,	3,210	1877,	6,088

XI.

THE COURTS.—PUBLIC LIBRARY.

Along with the wheat cometh the tares. And so it was with the first comers to the new city. Violent and wicked men had to be restrained and punished. Town governments in their adminis'ra'ion of justice were too slow-going coaches to take care of victims that which had to be confined in lockups from night to night. Therefore early as 1848, a Police Court was organized and Judge William Stevens of North Andover, was appointed Judge. This well remembered man occupied the bench from that year, 1848, to 1877, when he resigned on account of loss of eye sight. During his term the following gentlemen were consecutively clerks: Wm. H. P. Wright, Edgar J. Sherman, Henry L. Sherman, Charles E. Briggs, Jesse G. Gould, and H. F. Hopkins, the latter who still fills the position, having been recorder there since 1874.

After Judge Stevens retired the place was filled for about a year by associate Justice, W. H. P. Wright, when Judge N. W. Harmon received the appointment of Judge and assumed the duties May 1st, 1877.

On the 4th of January, 1878, Judge Stevens was stricken by apoplexy and died in a few hours. He was buried in North Andover, a committee of the Lawrence bar being chosen to attend his funeral. On the next return day, January 22d, appropriate resolutions were presented in the Police Court and entered on the records. Ad-

JUDGE WM. STEVENS.

dresses were made by District Attorney Sherman, A. C. Stone, C. U. Bell, W. L. Thompson, W. S. Knox, A. R. Sanborn, E. T. Burley, W. J. Quinn, and Judge N. W. Harmon. The present associate justices are W. Fisk Gile and C. U. Bell.

The Supreme Court has no session here. The Superior Court holds civil and criminal sessions.

PUBLIC LIBRARY.

The history of the Free Public Library of this city dates in one sense from the beginning of the town. The Franklin Library Association was chartered by the Legislature of 1847, and in July of that year Hon. Abbott Lawrence gave to the library the sum of one thousand dollars for the purchase of "such scientific and other works as will tend to create good mechanics, good christians and good patriots." Captain Charles H. Bigelow was the first President of the Association. In 1847 Mr. Lawrence died. He left by his will $5000 more for the Franklin Library. The price of shares was ten dollars, with an annual assessment of two dollars, and on these terms the library was open to anybody. Finding the price of the shares too high, the Association lowered the terms in 1853 to five dollars, and the assessment to one dollar, and in 1857 the library was thrown open to anybody who was willing to pay one dollar for its privileges. Even this small sum proved a barrier, and in 1868 the library was offered to the City Government to be used as a Public Library, but the offer was declined. In 1852, Hon. Daniel A. White, of Salem, left a fund, the income of which should be appropriated to a course of Lectures free to the industrial classes of Lawrence and for the purposes of a library. The White Fund Lectures are the result of that liberal bequest, and the rest of the income has materially aided the library. In 1872 the Association again offered their 4000 volumes and nearly $3000 to the city for a Free Library, and this time the offer was accepted, the trustees of the White Fund also proposing to contribute $1000 the first year and an annual sum afterward. July 2d, 1872, the Council established the Free Public Library of Lawrence. Shortly afterward the Agricultural Library, an association of Lawrence and Methuen gentlemen, transferred their books to the city library through the instrumentality of John C. Dow. August 29th, the trustees chose William I. Fletcher, Librarian. Mr. Fletcher resigned in March, 1874, and the present Librarian, Frederic H. Hedge, Jr., took charge of the library May 16th, 1874. The whole number of volumes in the library at this writing, including duplicates, is 18,000, exclusive of duplicates, 16,400.

NATHAN W. HARMON,

Judge of Police Court; office at Police Court Building; residence, 349 Haverhill St. Born in New Ashford, this State, 1813. Read law with the late Judge Byington, commencing practice in 1838 at Lanesboro and Adams, where he remained nine years. Was at one time law-partner with the late Ex-Gov. Briggs. Came to Lawrence June 11th, 1847. Judge Harmon has held numerous city offices, and has been a member of the school committee under town and city organization. Was in the lower house of legislature, 1857, in the senate, 1873, and commissioner under the bankrupt law of 1841. He has been a director of the Essex Savings Bank from the first. Appointed assistant assessor of Internal revenue in 1862, holding the position nine years. Was appointed judge, May 8th, 1877. Married Cornelia C. Briggs, 1841; has four children.

XII.

WATER WORKS—FIRE DEPARTMENT—NAVIGATION.

The Legislature of 1848 incorporated John Tenney, of Methuen, Alfred Kittredge, of Haverhill, and Daniel Saunders of Lawrence, and their associates, as the Lawrence Aqueduct Company, with a capital of $50,000, empowering them to take water from Hackett's pond in Andover, and convey it for distribution and use in Lawrence. The scheme was found to be impracticable and abandoned. The subject of a water supply continued to be more or less agitated, but nothing was done till 1871, when a number of citizens petitioned the City Council to take some steps to provide the city with a supply of pure water. The petition received favorable action, and Mayor S. B. W. Davis, Alderman James Payne, and President A. C. Stone, H. J. Couch, and Cyrus Williams of the Common Council were appointed a committee to make investigation of the subject matter, have the results arrived at recorded for the benefit of a future city government. The committee visited Lowell and Providence, made extended inquiries and decided that the water supply of Lawrence must either come from Haggett's Pond, North Andover Pond, Policy Pond in New Hampshire, or the Merrimac River, and the committee unhesitatingly recommended the latter.

In 1872 an act was obtained from the Legislature authorizing the city to take water from the river at any point in Lawrence or Methuen, and convey it through pipes into and about the city. The act was submitted to the voters of Lawrence, and was accepted by a vote of 1298 to 830, wards one and six giving majorities against it. A joint special committee on water was appointed from the City Government, consisting of Aldermen James Payne and James A. Treat, and President L. D. Sargent, H. J. Couch and George W. Russell from the Common Council to obtain surveys, plans and estimates of the cost of works needed to furnish the city with a suitable supply of pure water. This committee was allowed $8000 or less. Mr. Payne was made Chairman of the Committee. Mr. L. F. Rice of Boston, was engaged to make a preliminary survey. The committee reported that the advantages of the Merrimac for a water supply were so obvious that the passage of an ordinance creating a Board of Water Commissioners was warmly recommended.

In April 1873, Mayor Tarbox approved an ordinance creating a Board of Water Commissioners, and on the 8th of May, Wm. Barbour, Patrick Murphy, and Morris Knowles were created Water Commissioners. Mr. Barbour was made Chairman and Mr. Murphy Secretary. The Commissioners gave their attention as to the best system of distribution. The Holly or direct system had many friends and gave much satisfaction. The Commissioners finally decided to combine the Holly system and the Reservoir system, the former for fire purposes, and the latter for all general purposes of supply. Walter F. McConnell, of Boston, was engaged as Chief Engineer, and Baldwin Coolidge and Charles H. Littlefield as Assistants. James P. Kirkwood, of Brooklyn, was engaged as Consulting Engineer. Surveys were at once begun on the farm of Samuel Ames, where the Pumping Station and Filter Galleries are located, and on Bodwell's Hill where is the Reservoir.

MOULTON BATCHELDER,

City Marshal; office at Police Station. Residence, 18 Bradford St. Has been in Lawrence twenty-two years. Born at Plainfield, Vt., Dec. 7, 1836; has one child. His early life was spent upon a farm. For six years prior to 1862 he was watchman at the Washington Mills, at which time he enlisted in Co. C, 40th Mass. Reg't. Commissioned first-lieutenant in the 6th Reg't in 1864. Returned to Lawrence and was appointed on the police force, serving in various positions until 1873, when for two years he was keeper at the house of correction in this city. In 1875 was assistant marshal till July, when he was appointed marshal. Was marshal in 1876 day officer in 1877, and was again appointed marshal in 1878.

The lowest bid for constructing the reservoir was from J. B. Dacey & Co. of Boston, and Patrick Kiernan of Chelsea, and they were given the contract, breaking ground November 12th, 1873. But little was done that winter, but in the March following work was resumed. The contract called for the completion of the reservoir by the first day of October, 1875, but it was not quite completed at that time.

The water is pumped from the river by two of I. P. Morris & Co's engines, and is discharged into a force main thirty inches in diameter laid in the center of Ames street, extending to the reservoir, a distance of five thousand feet. Emery's Hill was tunnelled for a distance of 900 feet, the north end of the tunnel being a few feet south of Lowell street. The tunnel is six feet high, seven feet wide, egg shaped, with flattened bottom, and is built of hard burned brick laid in hydraulic cement, with a well or man-hole at either end to give free access, and to enable pipe to be lowered, should repairs be necessary. The force main is carried across Haverhill street just east of the house of Asa M. Bodwell, and enters the reservoir bank at the northwest corner. It goes through this bank to a point opposite the centre of the middle bank, where it turns and is carried along the middle bank to the overfall where it is turned upwards and the water is discharged, the stream being turned at will into either basin of the Reservoir. The Reservoir is of rectangular form, 730 feet long and 411 feet wide, and has a total capacity of 40,000,000 gallons when full. It is twenty-five feet deep. Each basin is 263 feet by 300 feet, measured on the bottom on the line of the skewbacks.

The street mains are all of cast iron pipe, and range from six to thirty inches in diameter. The main line of distribution is in Haverhill street, where a thirty inch pipe is laid to Broadway, then a twenty-four inch pipe to Hampshire street, and thence one of twenty inches to the Common, where it is still further reduced to sixteen inches, and at Jackson street the pipe is further reduced to twelve inches as far as the Spicket Bridge, where a ten inch pipe is used in Beach street till it meets the ten inch main in Prospect street. This is the main line of distribution, but there is another by which the water may be taken from the Reservoir through Ames, Canal, Water and Lawrence streets.

Besides the duplicate Reservoir distribution, the plan of direct pumping is added as a perfect guaranty of unbroken water supply, and for the purpose of extinguishing fires. The latter feature. however, has not as yet been tested. It is not known at this writing whether the mains would bear the strain of forcing water through them directly from the pumps with a pressure supplied for fire purposes, though the Reservoir pressure alone is sufficient in most places to enable the fire department to do good service with hose directly attached to the hydrants; in the future they will be more fully developed. The Lowry hydrant is in use. It is a flush hydrant, and is set, wherever practicable, in the streets directly over the main, and in fact is a part of the main. The salaries of the commissioner who put in the works and the pay of the inspectors, laborers, engineers and staff amounted to $63,128.54; travelling expenses, $4,264.41; cost of distributing reservoir, $275,151.44; pumping station, $161,923.30; engines and boilers, $116,851.51; pipe laying, $76,480.17; pipes, etc., $374,558.23; tunnel, $22,357.88; furniture, rent, etc., $1,998.78; engineers' instruments, $1,462.71; legal expenses, $585.00; stationery, $506.60; drawing materials, $502.22; printing and advertising, $1,449.89; house services, $10,191.02; land damages, $27,000; general construction, $20,940.05; maintenance, $4,719.34. Some unpaid bills swelled the total cost to $1,192,967.84.

May 9th, the term of office of the commissioners expired and they made a final report to the City Council. The care of the works is now vested in a Water Board consisting of Milton Bonney, President, R. H. Tewksbury, N. P. H. Melvin, Albert R. Field, David T. Porter. The Superintendent is Henry W. Rogers, Registrar, Geo. A. Durrell.

WILLIAM E. HEALD,

Chief Engineer of Lawrence Fire Department; office at Washington 5 Engine House, Lowell St.; residence, No. 330 Haverhill St. Born at Temple, N. H., 1839. Has resided in Lawrence since 1860. Learned the bottling business at Lynn, where he worked during 1855 and 1856. Worked in Salem at the same business during 1857, 1858 and 1859. Carried on the bottling business in Lawrence from 1860 to 1877, under the firm name of Wm. E. Heald & Co., 34 Hampshire St. Married Lucinda A. Jordan of Waltham, Me., in 1865; has one child. Joined the fire department in 1861; was assistant foreman several years and was upon the board of fire engineers in 1873, 1874, 1875, 1876 and the present year.

At this writing there have been laid about 2,500 service pipes. The number of water takers on the first of January last was 5,739. The corporations comprising the Lawrence Reservoir Association are supplied with city water at sixty dollars per million gallons. The bonded water debt of Lawrence is $1,300,000, and it is hoped that in a few years the number of takers will have become so much increased, and the cost of maintenance reduced so that the water works will become self-sustaining. Even if it should not quite do this, the citizens have abundant cause for congratulation that they have a generous supply of pure water.

FIRE DEPARTMENT.

Two employes of the Merrimac Machine Shop, Thomas Scott and N. S. Bean, were foremost in giving to the world the steam fire engine. It took some time for the public to find out the merit of the invention, but this was discovered at last and gladly accepted. The first one built here was called the Lawrence, and this was purchased by the city of Boston. The Amoskeag Company bought the invention, and the machines of that company are now too well known to need mention.

The first fire engine in use in Lawrence was the Essex, bought by the Essex Company, and manned by workmen in their employ, Mr. Henry Goodell foreman. The Essex was soon followed by machines of larger capacity, and by hose and hook and ladder companies, until at the introduction of the steam fire engine, the department was well equipped. In 1866 the city had four engines, with 6000 feet of hose. The department has now five steam fire engines, and one hook and ladder company. Each company has a separate hose carriage instead of having its hose pulled along behind as formerly. The water works now enable the department to do good service with hose directly attached to the hydrants. The pumping system is intended to give force enough to largely dispense with the engines, but this has not yet been effected. When the pipes have been subjected to pressure to see if they will bear the necessary force, this feature of the water works will be utilized. The pressure, however, from the reservoir alone is found useful. The fire engineers for 1878 are Wm. E. Heald, Albert Emerson and J. B. Campbell.

July 31st, 1869, was completed the Fire Alarm Telegraph. It was erected by Mr. Stevens, of Boston, at a cost of $8000 to the city. This has added materially to the efficiency of the department. Since that time the wires have been considerably extended, and many new alarm boxes have been put up to better convenience the people in giving prompt alarms. There are at present thirty-two fire alarm boxes, and the numbers now range from box 2 to box 51.

NAVIGATION.

The year 1877 marked the greatest advance yet made in navigating the Merrimac. In June 1848, the steamer Lawrence, Capt. Shepard, came up from Newburyport with a delegation from that place and adjoining towns. Since that time sundry efforts have been made to navigate the river, but with little success. Gen. Butler's efforts a few years ago to remove obstructions met with some success, and last year Mr. E. M. Boynton took hold of the matter with great energy, and made a marked advance. Many obstructions were removed, boats built for transporting coal, lands leased of the Essex Company for a landing place and coal yard, and several thousand tons of coal were delivered in this city direct from Newburyport before winter set in.

This year there have been numerous drawbacks to the enterprise. The channel at Mitchell's Falls proved to be neither deep enough or wide enough to guarantee safe transportation and efforts are still being made to improve it. Serious doubts are still entertained as regards utilizing the river for the carrying of freights, but it is more than probable that ere long a safe and available route will be opened from this city to the sea for the conveyance of passengers and pleasure parties.

ALBERT EMERSON,

Blacksmith, 341 Common St.; residence, 61 Tremont St. Has been in Lawrence twenty-four years. Was born in Dover, N. H. in 1831. Learned his trade and worked in Dover three years. Came to Lawrence in 1854 and engaged in business under the firm name of Bryant & Emerson, the partnership continuing seven years. Mr. Emerson has carried on business at his present location since then. Married Emeline E. Lord of South Berwick, Me., in 1851; has six children. Attends the Unitarian church. Was a member of the common council in 1861–2, alderman in 1863 and 1867, a member of the board of fire engineers in 1869, and is a member of the Board of Engineers the present year.

XIII.

ORDERS AND SOCIETIES.

No one thing perhaps shows the hand of human progress more than the increase of societies and organizations for the practice of the principles of benevolence and charity. Most of these organizations are private to the extent of having peculiar signs and grips—trade marks to prevent the intrusion of the uninitiated and scandal-monger,—but none of them requiring any obligation that in any way contravenes with civil or religious liberty. Among the oldest of these are the Free Masons, who claim an antiquity that dates back to the days of King Solomon. True, Masonry did exist in the early ages of the world. The building of temples required skilled labor. It was a branch of industry peculiar to itself. A workman upon these buildings must be familiar with every tool known to the masons' art, hence those competent to ply this vocation early found the need of organization, for to find continuous employment they must needs migrate from state to state and country to country. The organization became powerful and strong. But nowhere in the records given to posterity from the earliest date down to the seventeenth century of the Christian era is there found any account of a secret organization being long in existence and flourishing, that had for a corner stone the amelioration of mankind through that heaven born principle, charity. Secret societies, for divers purposes, have flourished to some extent in all ages, but as they at present exist the main idea is modern. They grow as civilization, education and religion pave the way. As superstition gives way to reason men learn more and more of that stereotyped phrase "the fatherhood of God and brotherhood of man." Societies now take root and grow founded solely upon the fraternal side of man's nature. Without contingent or sinking fund, they pay thousands of dollars to friends of deceased members with even more promptness and certainty than that of ordinary business firms. And these fraternal organizations are not alone confined to the male portion of society. Women are organizing on an equal basis with the men and are paying money into benefit funds, to be used in evening up the home comforts of the abodes of sickness and death with that of their own. It has long been held that women were a failure as organizers, not possessing the requisites by nature. But be this as it may they have ever been accredited with a desire to know all the secrets, and a little incident connected with the early history of our city may be cited here :—

To Ward Six belongs the honor of convening the first secret society meeting held in the city limits. There were a few masons living on the original territory, then Andover. This territory had been known for a hundred years as the "Moose Country." There were not over a dozen buildings in what is now Ward Six. There were the four houses that stood on the corner of Broadway and Andover streets, viz.: the Webster House, the Saunders house, Plumley house, and the house now occupied by Mr. Bunker.

On the Lowell road, about forty rods west of the Turnpike were two houses owned respectively by Mr. Caleb Richardson and Theodore Poor, and half a mile further west, a few rods apart, the house of Theodore Barnard and another dwelling house. A half mile beyond this was the house of Major Benjamin Stevens, and upon the road leading to West Andover was the house of Capt. James Stevens.

D. F. ROBINSON,

Manufacturer of Machine Card Clothing, 620 Essex St. Residence, 268 Haverhill St. Came to Lawrence in April, 1847. Born at Fremont, N. H., Dec. 1829. Commenced business April, 1857, and has continued it until the present time. Married Eliza Ann Norris, 1851; and has one child. Is connected with the Second Baptist Church, and is superintendent of its Sunday School. Was a member of the common council in 1866. For many years leader of the Lawrence Brass Band.

In the extreme southwest part of the ward was the house of Mr. Goldsmith, and on a road leading from Frye Village to what is now North Andover, was a house known far and near as the "White Dog House," so called from the fact that in early days no rum was allowed to be sold in Andover, and to evade the law, the proprietors of this house procured two diminutive white lap dogs, and charged for showing the dogs, throwing the "blackstrap" in. The thirsty very cheerfully paid for seeing the dogs, and tradition has it, that they just as cheerfully accepted the accompanying bonus. West of Turnpike, a little distance south of the Lowell road, was the Moses Town's house. A part of the chambers of this house were used by St. Mathew Lodge of Free and Accepted Masons, as a Lodge room, and in order to make an ante-room, quilts were hung across the room, thus partitioning it off. Mr. Town's servant girl being like her mother Eve, blessed with an inordinate curiosity, one evening secreted herself behind the quilts, in order, if possible, to obtain the secrets of the order. In this position she was discovered by the Tyler, and it is borne upon the archives of the Lodge that the damsel made but three steps from her place of concealment to the bottom of the stairs, and she shunned the company of Free Masons for ever after. This was the first Masonic Lodge room in what is now Lawrence.

Though women are still precluded from the secrets of Masonry the Order ranks first as a secret one, its age if nothing else giving it priorty.

Grecian Lodge, the oldest Lodge in the city dates from the 14th of December, 1825. It was started in Methuen. In 1838 the charter was surrendered, to be re-organized in this city in 1847. The semi-centennial was observed in 1875, and the historian was Charles H. Littlefield. The present officers are M. M. Chandler, Master; Chas. H. Littlefield, Secretary; J. R. Simpson, Treasurer.

Tuscan Lodge commenced work December 29th, 1862. The following May a charter was granted, and it has continued successful and prosperous since that time. Wm. Fisher, Master; Frank O. Kendall, Secretary; Rufus Reed, Treasurer.

Phœnician Lodge was instituted November 5th, 1870, and has been quite successful in making new members. The present officers are, Andrew C. Stone, Master; C. H. Moore, Secretary; S. M. Stedman, Treasurer.

There are three organized bodies in the higher order of Masonry. The Council was chartered in 1868. Mt. Sinai Royal Arch Chapter was chartered October, 1867, and Bethany Commandery Knights Templar in 1864. The whole number belonging to the Masonic Order in the city is over 800.

ODD FELLOWS.

Another powerful secret Order is the Odd Fellows. They also number in the city about 800 members, having three subordinate Lodges and two Encampments. The cardinal principles of the Order are Friendship, Love and Truth, and a feature of the beneficiary part of the Order is that the Lodges pay to sick members weekly benefits, not as a charity but as a right, quarterly dues being assessed upon the membership to keep the fund good. They take the name of Odd Fellows because it was odd at the time the Order was started sixty years ago, for men to band themselves together for such a work of love. The basis upon which the Independent Order of Odd Fellows is founded is peculiarly American, though Orders by the same name have had an existence in the Old World. Odd Fellowship was comparatively new in this country in 1845–46, though many comers to the new city had been initiated into the mystic tie.

In 1847 United Brothers Lodge was established, but owing to an *expose* of the work shortly after, and a general distrust about that time against all secret societies, for several years few new members were

ODD FELLOWS BUILDING.

added. Ten years later its beneficent workings became more and more visible, old prejudices softened and there has been a steady stream of slow but healthy additions ever since. Three years ago the members erected the fine building corner of Essex and Lawrence streets for their especial use, and it is a monument for the stability and strength of the Order. The first story is used for stores, the second for the Public Library, and the upper portion for Lodges and Encampments. Officers United Brothers Lodge, Thomas Hadfield, N. G.; J. O. Battershill, Secretary: A. H. Poulson, Treasurer. Num-of members, 330.

Monadnock Lodge was instituted in 1867, with fifteen charter members. It has had a prosperous career throughout. A ten years' history of this Lodge has been published this season making a handsome volume, compiled by C. B. Smith, a P. G. of the Lodge. The officers are Wm. K. Foster, N. G.; H. M. Chadwick, Secretary; Wm. F. Birtwell, Treasurer. It has 267 members.

Lawrence Lodge was instituted in 1869. It has had a steady and healthy growth since its organization. The officers are James Patterson, N. G.; John Edwards, Secretary; L. H. Benson, Treasurer. Membership 201.

There are two Encampments, higher branches of Odd Fellowship. These are the Kearsarge and Lawrence, there being about 200 members in the city that have taken the patriarchal degree.

The Knights of Pythias is a secret Order having for its object the care of sick and distressed brothers, and they also have an additional degree, recently adopted, whereby a certain sum, one, two or three thousand dollars is paid to relatives of deceased members as they may elect at the time of taking the degree. Quindaro Lodge has a membership of 100, being chartered in 1870. The officers are, Amos Southwick, C. C.; G. H. Robinson, V. C.; H. F. Hildreth, Keeper of Records and Seal.

WILLIAM WALLACE COLBY,

Undertaker. Place of business at 286 Common St.; residence, 254 Jackson St. Has been in Lawrence since November, 1849. Was born in Eaton, (now Madison) N. H. Received a common school education, spending his early life on a farm. Married Elizabeth A. F. George, Nov. 26, 1840; has nine children. Attends the Free Baptist church, and has been deacon since 1849. Commenced business at Haverhill, manufacturing shoes, 1838-1849. Came to Lawrence in the latter year, and worked at manufacturing sash and blinds for several years. Mr. Colby was a member of the common council for 1864-5. Superintendent of cemetery, 1871-2, and for the past four years has been in the furnishing and undertaker's business.

In 1875, Merrimack Lodge, Knights of Honor, was instituted. This was the first secret Order that had insurance as a chief pillar. Each member in this Order upon taking the third degree is assessed a certain sum to assist in forming a benefit fund to be used to the extent of paying $2,000 at the death of each member. This fund created by all the subordinate Lodges is managed by the Supreme Treasurer, who has jurisdiction over the Lodges throughout the country. The officers of Merrimack Lodge are T. F. Tucker, Dictator; H. A. Harris, Reporter; N. H. Berry, Treasurer. Membership, 180. The plan worked so admirably that a second Lodge of the Knights of Honor was instituted in the spring of 1877. It was given the name of Adelphic Lodge and has at present a membership of 125. The Officers are D. M. Spooner, Dictator; A. C. Curtis, Reporter; C. F. Crocker, Treasurer.

Another Order of a similar nature was started in this city the present year managing an insurance fund the same as the Knights of Honor, known as Knights of the Golden Cross. Women are admitted on equal terms with males and though a few months since organization it has a membership in the city of about 300. The officers of Olive Commandery are H. A. Wadsworth, Commander; A. J. French, Treasurer.

The Royal Arcanum is still another Order that pays $3,000 upon the death of any member and the fund is created by assessments when the treasury runs low. The officers of Lawrence Council are C. A. Metcalf, Commander; N. H. Berry Treasurer. Members, 100.

There are also in the city two Lodges of Forresters, two of the Ancient Order of Shepherds, one of Orangemen, and several temperance organizations that are secret to the extent of admitting none bnt members to regular meetings, and are founded upon the principles of mutual relief and assistance.

XIV

MINOR INDUSTRIES—CORPORATE AND INCORPORATE.

ARCHIBALD WHEEL COMPANY.

This corporation has a history dating from 1871. It was formed for the manufacture of iron hubbed wheels for express, truck and team wagons, carts, portable engines, steam fire engines and hose carriages, by the Archibald Patent Press Process. These wheels have been adopted by the largest and best known manufacturers of wagons and steam fire engines in the United States, and also by the government in quartermaster and ordinance wagons, after years of severe and patient trial in competition with all other wheels known. At this establishment the lumber is sawed from the log, planed and formed into spokes and felloes, and before use, is piled in the store house, 80 by 60 feet in dimensions, where it is allowed to remain and season from eighteen months to two years before put to use. The buildings of the company are three in number, the main workshop 100 by 45 feet, the store-house and boiler-house. The capital stock of the company is $60,000, and when run to its fullest capacity the works furnish employment to twenty persons. The officers of the corporation are: J. C. Hoadley, President; Hezekiah Plummer, Treasurer; and E. A. Archibald, Superintendent.

EBEN EDWARDS FOSTER,

Boot and Shoe Dealer at 26 So. Broadway. Residence, 19 Farnham St., South Lawrence. Has been a resident twenty-three years. Born in Windham, N. H., Feb. 15, 1827. His father being a manufacturer of leather and leather goods, Mr. Foster naturally became connected at an early age with the same business, and has followed it nearly all his life. Educated in the public schools and academy at Manchester, N. H., he early developed mechanical talent, choosing the manufacture and sale of leather goods; during the war was successful. Has a good business record, always paying one hundred cents on a dollar. Married Miss M. A. Stearns, Aug. 26, 1849, for his first wife, who died in 1876; his second wife is Mrs. A. L. Hamilton; has three daughters. Is connected with the South Congregational Church. Has been a deacon in both the Eliot and Central Congregational churches. In 1866 built the large manufactory at the corner of Methuen and Franklin Sts., letting power for mechanical purposes.

MCKAY SEWING MACHINE ASSOCIATION.

This Association was formed in 1864, and purchased the lot of land, 45,157 square feet, upon which the manufactory now stands. A main building, three stories high, brick, 152 feet long by 40 wide, an L, one story in height, 147 by 40 feet, and a fire proof building for the preservation of model machines, gauges and special tools, in dimensions 17 by 25 feet, were then erected, and operations were commenced in 1865. Since that time, the business having steadily increased, an additional L, three stories in height and 17 by 25 feet, has been erected. The Association new employs 175 workmen in the manufacture of McKay sewing machines for shoes, McKay & Bigelow heeling machines, McKay metallic fastening standard screw machines, Goodyear & McKay sewing machine and McKay channellers. None of these machines are sold, but are leased upon royalty, and their revenue is rapidly increasing. Mr. Thomas Scott is Superintendent of the works. In 1877 the Association disposed of 298 McKay sewing machines, 149 McKay channelers, 140 McKay & Bigelow heeling machines, 79 metallic fastening screw machines, and 56 Goodyear & McKay sewing machines.

LAWRENCE GAS COMPANY.

In 1847 the Bay State and Atlantic Mills and the Essex Company were formed into an association and erected suitable buildings for the manufacture of gas for their own use. In 1849 the association disbanded, and a stock company, known as the Lawrence Gas Company, was formed, and February 14th, 1849, secured an act of incorporation. The capital at this time was $40,000, and the company began lighting the streets and introducing their pipes into private residences. Gradually since that time the capital has been increased, additional buildings erected, and pipes laid until now hardly an accepted street in the city which has not a number of street lamps burning gas. The capital at the present time is $400,000. There have been laid since 1849, twenty-nine miles of main pipe, 17 miles of service, and 2100 metres set. The officers of the corporation are, J. J. Storrow, President; Gardner P. Gates, Treasurer; Geo. D. Cabot, Agent; A. C. Tenney, Clerk.

RUSSELL PAPER COMPANY.

This corporation was organized in April, 1864, with a capital of $100,000. Here is manufactured writing, book and manilla papers, in all of which the company has been very fortunate, and have achieved marked success. The mill property constitutes four large buildings with the latest improved machinery. Two hundred and fifty persons are employed here, and ten tons of paper, on an average, are manufactured daily. The officers are, William A. Russell, Treasurer, and George W. Russell, Superintendent.

FLYER AND SPINDLE WORKS.

In 1862, what is now known as the Lawrence Flyer and Spindle Works were started at the lower end of the canal. In 1867 a stock company was formed with a capital of $50,000, and these works, which for five years previous were controlled by private enterprise, became the property of a corporation. At present thirty persons are employed here in the manufacture of spinning flyers, spindles, spindle tubes and mill machinery. The officers of the corporation are, Joseph P. Battles, Treasurer, and H. P. Chandler, Agent.

LAWRENCE LUMBER COMPANY.

The Lawrence Lumber Company was incorporated in 1868, with a capital of $54,000. The business is the manufacture of wooden boxes, and every description and dimension of lumber. Forty persons are in the employ of this company. This company does more

JOHN WELLES PORTER,

Keeper of Livery and Sale Stable, corner of Lawrence and Methuen Sts. Residence, 107 Garden St. Has been in Lawrence twenty-eight years. Was born in Lyman, N. H., June 17th, 1833. Married Miss Adeline A. Moore of Andover, Mass., Aug. 17th, 1853; has one son. Attends Grace church. Has been in the stable business since 1860. Was a member of the police department under the first city government, and was connected with that department for several years as policeman and constable. Was city marshal in '59, '62 and '63. also assistant mashal for several years, closing his official service with the year 1872.

than a mere local business, sending lumber and building material to all parts of the county. The annual business amounts to between two and three hundred thousand dollars. The officers are, Morris Knowles, President; Luther Ladd, Treasurer and Agent.

NATIONAL BANKS.

Bay State. Incorporated, 1847. Capital, $375,000. George L. Davis, President; Samuel White, Cashier.

Pemberton. Incorporated, 1854. Capital, $150,000. L. Sprague, President; J. M. Coburn, Cashier.

Lawrence. Incorporated, 1872. Capital, $300,000. A. W. Stearns, President; P. G. Pillsbury, Cashier.

Pacific. Incorporated, 1877. Capital, $100,000. J. H. Kidder, President; Wm. H. Jaquith, Cashier.

SAVINGS BANKS.

Essex. Incorporated, 1847. Joseph Shattuck, President; James H. Eaton, Treasurer.

Lawrence. Incorporated, 1870. Milton Bonney, President: Wm. R. Spalding, Treasurer.

Broadway. Incorporated, 1872. John Fallon, President; Gilbert E. Hood, Treasurer.

RAILROADS.

The year 1848 brought Lawrence into direct connection with Boston, Lowell and Salem. Finding that there was to be a city here, the managers of the Boston and Maine Railroad changed their location between Andover and North Andover, running the road round to South Lawrence, and on the 28th of February the road ran their passenger trains across the bridge to the station on the north side of the river. July 2d, 1848, the Lowell and Lawrence ran free trains and carried over 8000 people. The Essex Railroad was opened from Lawrence to Salem, September 4th, 1848; the Manchester and Lawrence road was opened in October, 1849. Last year the Lowell and Lawrence Railroad obtained permission of the Railroad Commissioners to cross the Boston and Maine tracks at grade in South Lawrence, and the Mayor and Aldermen granted permission to the road to extend its tracks across the river and through the Atlantic yard to Essex street. The bridge is now built. The Superior Court having enjoined the Lowell and Lawrence road from taking the location of the Boston and Maine at South Lawrence to come in on, the Legislature passed a special act on the request of the Railroad Commissioners to give them permission to adjust the difficulty.

As the population increased the need of a Horse Railroad grew apparent, and in 1867 a single track was laid from Methuen to the Paper Mills in Lawrence, Subsequently the line was extended to North Andover, and in 1876 the track was laid to South Lawrence. The latter proved to be the best of the line, but even to the last there were found stockholders who were sure it would not pay. This year the company has petitioned the Mayor and Aldermen for permission to build a double track in Essex street. The President of the corporation is Wm. A. Russell; Treasurer, James H. Eaton.

Besides the corporate bodies to which Lawrence is indebted largely for its growth, there have sprung up within the past twenty-five years a number of minor manufactories, controlled by private individuals which have added in no small measure to the material prosperity of the city. Among these are the following:

EXPRESSES.

The first Boston and Lawrence Express was that of Stevens & Abbott. In July, 1851, Mr. Abbott retired, and the firm was Stevens & White, well known as "Sam" White. In March 1852, White retired and was followed by J. A. Stevens. In September, 1852, Stevens was succeeded by P. B. Putney. In December, 1852, Mr. Putney associated with himself J. George, of Concord, N. H., under the firm name of Putney & George. The latter had been employed by the U. S. and Canada Express and brought with him a good knowledge of the business. The firm was dissolved by the death of Mr. George, May 5th, 1869. In 1870 the firm of Cogswell & Co., was organized, Mr. Cogswell taking Mr. Lewis Saunders as a partner, and the firm has since done a large business. In 1859 three horses did the entire work of the firm. They now employ about thirteen horses, and twenty-five men.

Messrs. Abbott & Co., also do a thriving express business, running between this city and Boston, also to Methuen. The business of this office was begun about twenty years ago by W. F. Cooper, being succeeded in 1871 by J. G. Abbott. It requires ten men and five horses to do the work.

E. Davis & Son's Iron Foundry has been operation since 1863. The buildings connected with the works are four in number, and afford capacity for the employment of thirty persons.

H. K. Webster & Co.'s Grain Mill was built in 1868, and at present employs eight persons. The mill is 120 by 30 feet, and connected with the mill property are two store houses. The capacity is placed at 1200 bushels of meal per day.

Webster & Dustin, Machinists, have been in business at their present location, Canal street, since October, 1876. They now employ twelve persons, and manufacture mill machinery, shafting, pulleys, gearing, etc.

N. W. Farwell & Son's Bleachery is one of the new enterprises which have sprung up at South Lawrence during the past year. Operations in dyeing and bleaching were commenced January, 1878, and at present the works give employment to sixty persons.

The Hosiery Mill, Canal street, until recently run by Carter & Wilson, commenced operations in 1874. Three buildings are connected with the works and forty persons employed. The amount of production per day, is on an average, sixty dozen, the value of which is estimated at $150.

Carter & Rolan employ twelve hands in wool sorting and scouring for out-of-town dealers. Annually at this establishment half a million pounds of wool are handled.

F. W. McLanathan begun the business of Roll Covering in 1874, and at present employs five hands.

George A. Furguson started in Carriage Manufacture in Lawrence in 1867. Recently he erected a large brick building on Methuen street, where he now carries on the business and employs twelve tradesmen.

Edward Page, "the original Belt Manufacturer," is one of the pioneers of Lawrence, starting in business here in 1846. He now employs fifteen hands.

Stedman & Fuller have been in the Card Clothing business for the past quarter of a century, and when working to its fullest capacity the establishment gives employment to a dozen workmen.

Berry & Co.'s U. S. Steam Feed, is another of the more recent enterprises. By a lately patented apparatus grain is dried, cooked, and ground for feed. Five workmen are employed here.

The Broadway Cracker Bakery, J. H. Nichols, agent, employs eight persons in the manufacture of all kinds of crackers. Two hundred barrels of flour are used here monthly.

James W. Joyce has been engaged in Carriage Manufacture in Lawrence for the past twelve years. Twelve persons are employed here.

Butler's File Works have been in operation since 1854, now employ fifteen hands, and the productive capacity is 500 dozen files per month.

MARK MANAHAN,

Grocer, 106 Broadway, corner Salem street; residence corner Salem and Carver streets. Came to Lawrence 12 years ago, April 1866. Born at Deering, Hillsboro', Co., N. H. Worked on a farm in early life and had the advantages of a Common and High School education. Married April 1865, to Emily R. Stiles, of Middleton, Mass. Has three children. Attends South Congregational church. Mr. Manahan entered into partnership with his brother Harlan D, which still continues doing business under the firm name of M. & H. D. Manahan. This is the oldest grocery firm now doing business in South Lawrence. Was a member of the Common Council in 1869 and 1870, and at present is a member of the Board of Overseers of the Poor.

Robinson & Perkins, Card Clothing manufacturers, began business in Lawrence in 1857, and now employ a dozen persons. At this establishment from 8,000 to 10,000 sides of leather, and from twenty to twenty-five tons of wire are used annually. The annual production is from fifty to sixty thousand feet of card clothing.

Williams & Willson, Machinists, commenced in Lawrence fifteen years ago and employ fifteen hands.

J. E. Watts began in 1874 in the Brass Foundry Business. To this he has recently added the manufacture of steam and water regulators, of which he is the inventor. He furnishes employment to five persons.

The Merrimac Iron Foundry has been operated since 1854, now employs fifty hands, and has a productive capacity of 150 tons of castings per month.

The Lawrence Flour Mills, Davis & Taylor proprietors, grind annually about 125,000 bushels of wheat, turning out about 25,000 barrels of flour. About 250,000 bushels grains of other varieties are here ground annually. The mill has been in operation for ten years, and furnishes employment to twelve persons.

The Berkley Mills were moved to Lawrence in 1873, by Mr. Thos. Greenbank, the present owner. They are engaged in the manufacture of flannels of all grades; employ seventy-five persons, operate 2800 spindles and fifty-seven looms, and the productive capacity is 90,000 yards of flannel per month. Annually 300,000 pounds of wool are consumed here.

Alderman Thomas Clegg began the business of Reed and Loom Harness manufacturing in this city in 1852. Recently he has moved to the south canal where he has added the manufacture of Leather Board to his former business. Twenty-five hands are employed in the manufacture of reeds and loom harnesses, and fifteen in the leather board department. Upwards of 25,000 reeds and harnesses are produced annually at this establishment.

B. S. Hale & Son, since 1872 have engaged in the manufacture of fish line and patent laid cords at South Lawrence. They now employ eighteen hands.

Samuel Carter employs twelve workmen in jobbing and general machinery repairs. He has been in the business in this city since 1870.

Butler & Robinson's Yarn Mill has been in operation since 1863. At this mill is manufactured worsted yarns. Has 5,000 spindles, four sets of cards, five company machines, and 125 hands are employed.

Josslyn & Webster's Iron Foundry was started about ten years ago. Twenty persons are employed here, and upwards of sixty tons of castings are turned out monthly. Business now at this foundry is quite brisk.

Hayden's Leather Board Mill, formerly operated by George E. Davis has now been leased for a term of years by Allen, Jones & Co., of Boston, manufacturers of wood paper pulp and leather board. The capacity at present is one ton of leather board a day. Ten persons are now employed here. The mill has been in operation under various managements the greater part of the past ten years.

What is now known as Bacon's Paper Mill was formerly the property of the Lawrence Paper Company. About fifteen years ago it was purchased at auction sale by Messrs. James S. Monroe and J. A. Bacon, and by this firm operated for five years. Mr. Bacon then purchased his partner's right, and rebuilt the mill, adding machinery and making other improvements. One hundred and twenty operatives now manufacture, on an average, 120 tons of paper a month. George W. Seaverns is Superintendent of the mills.

Sprague & Co., Bobbin manufacturers, have been in the business since 1862. They employ 110 hands in the manufacture of bobbins and spools used in cotton and wool factories.

Armington & Simms, dealers and manufacturers of Portable Steam Engines. Employ fifty hands. The monthly production is $10,000.

Tower & Hadley's Coffee and Spice Mills, have been in operation since 1874. They furnish employment to five hands and do a yearly business varying from $40,000 to $50,000.

Albert Blood, Machinist, has been in business in this city since 1853. By the purchase of additional facilities his business has been greatly increased within the past few years. He now employs twenty hands.

Beach's Soap Company manufacture extensively the celebrated Beach's Washing Soap, doing a large business in the surrounding country. Employ twelve hands with a monthly production valued at $7,000.

Sargent's Steam Mill, L. D. Sargent, proprietor. Boxes, mouldings, gutters, and house finish, planning, etc. Employs twenty-three hands and produces 200,000 feet monthly.

T. A. Emmons manufactures Loom Harnesses. Employs sixty hands on custom work, fiilling orders for manufacturers in all parts of the country.

James Byrom manufactures Brass Castings of all kinds. Employs six hands.

Moses B. Ames & Co., Carriage Manufacturers, Lowell street. This is the oldest carriage repository in the city. John Gale was the original proprietor, Mr. Ames, his successor, engaging with him in the business fourteen years ago. Mr. Gale retired about four years ago. There are twenty men employed.

Stanley & Co., Brewers. This firm bought the brewery property on Oxford street about six years ago, and since that time have increased its capacity four or five times. Thirteen men were then employed at the establishment, while at present it requires sixty men to do the work. The product is stock and present use Ale and Lager Beer.

Allen Wilson, Oak street, has the oldest established bakery in the city. Employs twelve hands.

XV.

NOTABLE EVENTS, ETC.

The first calamity worthy of note which happened in the city was the accident at the dam on the 12th of October, 1847. At the time the accident occurred about 300 feet of the dam on the south side, and 100 feet on the north side of the river had been finished, the water meanwhile running over the unfinished part. The unfinished space was about 500 feet long, and it became necessary to shut out the water from this by a coffer dam. The timbers of the coffer dam were all in position and braced, as was supposed, securely, and workmen were engaged in putting down flash boards. Both Mr. L. M. Wright, who had charge of the wood work of the dam, and Captain Bigelow were present at the time and aiding, in all confidence as to the strength of the structure, in putting down plank after plank. In an instant that portion of dam upon which they were engaged, rose upon the surface of the water, and fifteen men were swept, amid the broken timbers, by the rush of the fearful flood upon the rocks twenty-five feet below. Capt. Bigelow and Mr. Wright were in a scow, and this swayed round in the current and passed over the dam. Just as she was making the plunge, two men leaped out and saved themselves upon that portion of the coffer dam which remained firm. Another man leaped from the stern of the boat directly into the falling current and escaped unhurt. The end of the scow plunged with terrible force upon the bed rock, sending its freight of men and tools with great velocity in the river. Capt. Bigelow came very near losing his life. He was badly injured, and was only saved by the utmost exertions of Mr. Wright. Two men were killed, two seriously injured, and three slightly injured. At the time of this accident every nerve was being exerted to raise the water to its proper level to supply power to the Bay State Mills, then nearly completed and ready in some parts for the machinery. Every person was looking forward to this desirable consummation with high hopes of future business, and the accident therefore felt as a personal as much as a public calamity.

The heaviest freshet was in April, 1852, when the highest pitch of water was ten feet upon the crest of the dam. This freshet washed out the abutment of the bridge and carried away the toll-house on the south side of the river. The water, at intervals, reached the wood work on the railroad bridge. The alarm in the city in anticipation of an overflow of the wing walls of the dam was very great, and so imminent was the danger in the estimation of the engineers of the Essex Company, that a train of cars and a large number of teams were run night and day in conveying earth for an embankment to protect the town. In 1863, the water reached nine feet or within one foot of great flood.

The greatest calamity that has yet befallen Lawrence was the fall of the Pemberton Mill. On the 10th of January, 1860, at thirteen minutes before five o'clock in the afternoon, the mill fell without a moment's warning. The building was five stories high, eighty-four feet wide, and two hundred and eighty feet long. The first story was devoted to weaving, the second to carding, the third to spinning, the fourth to carding, spinning and drawing-in, and the fifth to dressing, warping, spooling, winding and reeling. About seven hundred persons were at work in the mill when it fell. Mr. Chase, the agent, and Mr. Huse, one of the owners, were passing through the spinning room when a noise was heard, the mules stopped, and the building was seen to be falling. They stepped into a wing, and were saved. One hundred persons were killed. A large number were more or less injured, some of them for life. The scene after the fall was one of indescribable horror. Hundreds of men, women and children were buried in the ruins. Many of them assured their friends they were uninjured but imprisoned by the timbers about them. Others were dead or dying. Everybody worked as hard as possible to relieve the unfortunate ones till nearly ten o'clock at night, when saddest of all, a lantern broke and set the ruins on fire. In a few minutes the entire mass was a sheet of flames. Fourteen are known to have perished in the burning mass. The cause of the disaster is not known, but it is believed that there was a defective iron pillar in one of the upper rooms at the south end of the mill.

There have been three disturbances of the public peace, two of them serious. The first and least important one was the demolition of the "Black House," a low resort on Water street, in April, 1847. A more serious disturbance took place in 1854 between the Know Nothings and the Irish. It was reported that an Oak street Irishman had raised the American flag, union down. The anti-foreigners paraded the streets with bands and banners in the evening. On Common street, between Jackson and Newbury streets, the opposing forces met, when fists, stones, and even pistols were used. Fortunately, no one was killed though the house of the man who was said to have raised the flag was badly damaged. The city subsequently paid the bill.

The next and last riotous demonstration thus far, occurred in 1875, on the 12th of July. On that day, the anniversary of the battle of Boyne, was celebrated by the Orangemen of Lawrence by a pic-nic at Laurel Grove, in which they were joined by delegations from Lowell, Woburn, and Arlington. The Orangemen had been to the grove, the visiting lodges had been taken to Lowell by the steamer

CHASE PHILBRICK,

State Detective. Office, Schaake's Building; residence, 138 Broadway. Has been in Lawrence since 1863. Born at Sanbornton, N. H. 1823. Received a common school education and learned the stone cutter's trade, at which he worked till 1861. Was married in 1856; has three children. Enlisted as captain, in 1861, in the 15th Mass. Reg't, and was promoted to major, May, 1862; to lieutenant-colonel, Nov., 1862; discharged for disability, April, 1863. Was with the Army of the Potomac in the Peninsula Campaign and the battles of Ball Bluff, Second Bull Run, Anteitam and Fredericksburg. Col. Philbrick was City Marshal in 1864, 1865, 1866, 1867, 1868, 1869, 1870, 1872 and 1873; Street Commissioner, 1871; State Constable, 1874 and 1875; State Detective, 1876, 1877 and 1878.

City of Lawrence, and the steamer at five o'clock in the afternoon returned to this city with the Orangemen belonging here. At the Water street landing several hundred persons were assembled, and their jeers and words of derision indicated that there might be trouble. The Orangemen started down Essex street, not in procession. Some stones were thrown soon after leaving the boat, and near the Essex House somebody tore a regalia from one of the picnicers. The Orangemen flourished their pistols, and loud talk was heard on both sides. The Orangemen who had on their regalias sought shelter in the station house, and Mayor Tewksbury was sent for. The latter told the crowd that there must be order, and that every man would be protected in his rights. Two men hissed the Mayor and were arrested. The Mayor started into the streets with an escort of police consisting of officers Gammell, Dyson, Floyd and Corliss. Stones were thrown, Corliss and Dyson being hit. The Mayor and his escort kept on, the crowd growing more and more excited. Somebody in the crowd fired a pistol. The officers fired in return. About a dozen shots in all were fired. Arriving at the house of the commander of the Lodge, J. H. Spinlow, 71 Prospect street, a guard was stationed there and no further disturbance took place. Several persons were slightly injured. Since that time the Orangemen have paraded here, but met with no opposition.

THE CITY'S GROWTH.

Population.

1845 (estimated,)	150
1855	16,084
1865	21,723
1875	34,916
1878 (estimated,)	39,000

Valuation.

1847	$2,292,372
1850	5,577,944
1855	9,954,041
1860	10,586,023
1865	12,683,273
1870	17,912,500
1877	23,902,537

City Debt.

1847	$15,000
1850	98,325
1855	137,500
1860	172.233
1865	283,450
1870	413,889
1875	485,028
1877 (excluding water loan)	382,585

THE STREETS.

The streets of Lawrence are generally fifty feet wide. Essex street is eighty, Broadway sixty-six, Canal, Jackson, Appleton, Common and Haverhill, from Broadway to Spring street, sixty feet; Mechanic street is only forty feet. The highest elevation between Broadway and the Spicket is at the corner of Cross and Franklin streets which is seventy-five feet above the Essex Company's base line. At the corner of Essex and Lawrence streets it is thirty-eight feet above that line, and four feet higher than the crest of the dam.

OLD RESIDENTS' ASSOCIATION.

In order to preserve the facts pertaining to the history of Lawrence, an Old Residents' Association was formed December 22d, 1877, as follows: President, Daniel Saunders; Vice President, Robert H. Tewksbury; Executive Committee, W. H. P. Wright, William R. Pedrick, Nathaniel Ambrose, Nathan W. Harmon, Patrick Sweeney, Dr. Aaron Ordway, Mrs. Caroline L. Bartlett, Mrs. Abbie A. Wilcox, Mrs. Uretta E. McAllister, Mrs. Caroline E. Fay, Miss Katharine A. O'Keeffe, Miss Francis Paul; Historian, John R. Rollins.

THE PIONEERS.

Of the settlers in Lawrence during the early months of its history, few remain; during the first ten years of its existence hardly any one came here with a purpose of making it a permanent settlement; its growth from the desert had been so sudden, so mushroom-like; everywhere reigned such supreme disorder and incompleteness that it presented few attractions other than the advantages of its busy, bustling thrift and business opportunities; within the past half score of years this has changed; the character and permanence of a city established, its growth and future assured, it has become a place of homes instead of stopping places, and the former ever shifting character of its population is solidified into a permanence and stability eminently gratifying. But of the immigrants of 1845 to 1848, very few remain; of a dozen resident physicians in 1848, only three, Drs. Wm. D. Lamb, Isaac Tewksbury, and David Dana, now remain here in practice, although Dr. Blanchard, for some years absent, has since returned, engaging in business pursuits. Of an equal number of attorneys, only three, Daniel Saunders, Jr., Thomas A. Parsons and Ivan Stevens, remain, and not a single clergyman; of the merchants, less than a dozen, and of the entire population, not above a hundred are now resident in the city.

XVI.

LAWRENCE IN THE REBELLION.

---

* The first meeting of the City Council, to act upon matters connected with the war, was a special meeting held April 16th, 1861, at which the following preamble and resolutions were adopted :—

Whereas the President of the United States, in view of the dangerous Rebellion now existing in several of the Federal States, threatening alike the security and liberty of our homes, has seen fit to make a requisition upon the Governor of this Commonwealth for a certain number of troops to assist in quelling said Rebellion ; and as the two military companies of Lawrence comprise a portion of the Sixth Regiment of militia who, in obedience to said requisition, are now on their way to report themselves at headquarters ; therefore be it

Resolved, By the city of Lawrence, that the sum of five thousand dollars be, and hereby is, appropriated, to be used in case of need, to provide for the wants of those who comprise these companies, or their families.

Five thousand dollars additional were appropriated for the same purpose, May 16th, and in October following another appropriation of three thousand dollars was made.

On the 18th of April a petition of Daniel Saunders, Jr., and others, was presented to the City Council, asking an appropriation for the

* Schouler's History.

MELVIN BEAL,

Mechanic; residence, 213 Broadway. Has been in Lawrence nearly twenty-six years. Born at Guilford, Me., Oct. 31, 1832. Attended the common school and worked on a farm until sixteen. Married Emily M. Goodhue of Salem, N. H., Nov. 9, 1853; has one son. Attends the Universalist church. Left Maine in 1850, going to Pelham, N. H., and working at carding and spinning in a woolen mill until Oct. 1852, when he came to Lawrence and worked in the Bay State Mill as spinner and second hand of spinning till 1856, when he went painting, which he followed when not in the army till 1866, when he was appointed State Constable, which position he held for nine years. Councilman for Ward I, 1866; two years assistant and two years chief engineer of fire department; 20 years a fireman. Representative from 21st District in the legislature, 1878, and was a member of the military committee. Colonel of 6th Regt. M. V. M. For full military record see history of regiment.

purpose of equipping a regiment of volunteer militia; and five thousand dollars were appropriated for that purpose. At the same meeting the Mayor was requested to cause the national flag to be raised upon the flagstaff on Lawrence Common, "there to remain as a permanent evidence of our devotion to our country." April 24th, fifteen hundred dollars were appropriated "for the purchase of flannels and other materials asked for by the Ladies' Soldiers' Aid Society of Lawrence," to be made into articles for the use of the volunteers.

On the receipt of the news of the death of Sumner Henry Needham, who fell in Baltimore on the memorable 19th of April, and whose name has become historical as one of the first martyrs of the Rebellion, the following resolutions were passed by both branches of the City Government:—

Resolved, That to the afflicted relatives and friends of the dear departed, in this hour of their deep heart grief, we extend our tenderest sympathies; and, while we would not invade the sanctity of their sorrow, his loss to us, as a community, a people, and a nation, and the remembrance of the noble patriotism and holy devotion inspiring the mission in which he has fallen, throws upon our hearts the same cloud of sadness, and unites our grief to theirs.

Resolved, That in respect to the memory of the deceased this City Government will attend the funeral in a body; that we invite our fellow-citizens generally to join in paying a last tribute of respect to the departed, and we recommend the closing of all places of business in our city on the occasion of his interment.*

The city of Lawrence continued its activity in behalf of the great cause until the end of the war, making liberal appropriations of money to encourage recruiting, and for the payment of State aid to the families of volunteers, for which a special agent of the city was

* Mr. Tewksbury, the City Treasurer, writes: "In accordance with the resolves, the City Government attended the funeral in a body, with distinguished State officials, and a countless throng of citizens. He was buried from the City Hall, all business being suspended for the time, and the flags displayed at half mast, with general evidence of mourning on every hand. A suitable granite monument in the Lawrence Cemetery marks the last resting place of the martyr."

placed in charge. Each company belonging to the city, on its return from the front at the close of its term of service, was received "with fitting welcome and suitable demonstrations."

Lawrence furnished two thousand four hundred and ninety-seven men for the war, which was a surplus of two hundred and twenty-four over and above all demands. Ninety-two were commissoned officers. The whole amount of money appropriated and expended by the city on account of the war, exclusive of State aid, was one hundred and fifteen thousand six hundred and thirty dollars and ten cents, ($115,630.10).

The amount of money raised by the city during the four years of the war for State aid paid to the families of volunteers, and which was afterwards repaid by the Commonwealth, was as follows: In 1861, $14,524.05; in 1862, $52,555.52; in 1863, $58,153.48; in 1864, $45,000.00; in 1865, $22,000.00. Total amount, $192,233.05.

The "Ladies' Soldiers' Aid Society" of Lawrence continued their patriotic work during the continuance of the war. They held weekly meetings in the Common Council room in the City Hall, to make under-clothing, bandages, lint, and other articles, for the sick and wounded in the hospitals. They also contributed upwards of seven thousand dollars in cash, in various practical charities to the soldiers."

The history of the Sixth Regiment, which is so closely identified with this city was one of the most eventful of the war. The first to respond to the call for the country's safety, and the first to bleed in the mighty struggle. This regiment has the undisputed honor of first reaching Washington after the famous fight in Baltimore on the 19th of April, 1861.

As early as January 21st of that year the officers of the Sixth Regiment had authorized Colonel Jones to pledge the service of the Regiment to the government. Major B. F. Watson presented the resolution. On the 15th of April Gov. Andrew ordered Col. Jones

SMITH M. DECKER,

Grocer, 36 Amesbury St. Resides at 333 Haverhill St. Has been in Lawrence 18 years. Born in Swanton, Vt., 1843. Liberally educated at Franklin Academy, Vt. Has been in business at the present place 11 years. Firm name now Decker & Whittier; first three years was Decker & Andrews, the latter retiring on account of ill health. Col. Decker enlisted in 1862 in the 13th Vermont Regiment; commissioned 2d lieut., 1863. In 1864 enlisted in the 6th Mass. Regiment. Served as sergeant, 1st lieutenant and captain in Co. K of this regiment. July, 1872 was made lieutenant-colonel of the Sixth. Was mustered out at the re-organization, and appointed provost-marshal on the staff First Brigade. In 1877 was commissioned major of the Sixth Reg't, which position he at present holds.

to muster his command on Boston Common and proceed to Washington. Lawrence furnished two companies, I and F, and Lieut. Colonel B. F. Watson. Co. F, the "Warren Light Guard," was organized March 3d, 1855, and named in honor of General Joseph Warren. and Co. I, the "Lawrence Light Infantry," was organized in 1849. Company F was commanded by Capt. B. F. Chadbourne, Melvin Beal 2d lieutenant, Thomas J. Cate, 3d lieutenant, Jesse C. Silver, 4th lieutenant. Company I was commanded by Capt. John John Pickering, 1st lieutenant, D. S. Yeaton, 2d lieutenant, A. L. Hamilton, 3d lieutenant, E. H. Ellenwood, 4th lieutenant, Eugene J. Mason.

The regiment reached Philadelphia at midnight of the 18th, and trouble being feared in their passage through Baltimore, ammunition was distributed and orders given to the men that trouble might be expected. Baltimore is a city of 200,000 population, and at that time more than half of the population were rebels. People not acquainted with the railroad accommodations at Baltimore do not exactly understand the situation and how the fight came about. The cars from Philadelphia enter the city on the north side; here they are detatched from the locomotive and drawn through the city for two miles by horses to the Baltimore and Washington depot. The train containing the regiment consisted of eleven cars. Seven of them were hauled safely through. The remaining four containing the band, Co. C, and D, of Lowell, Co. I, of this city, and Co. L, of Stoneham, were started shortly after, but the infuriated mob becoming more determined, barricaded the track and would not allow them to proceed. These men then left the cars and proceeded to cross the city on foot to the depot for Washington, and it was at this time that the troops were fired upon, and one of the first that fell was Corporal Sumner H. Needham, of Co. I. He was born in Bethel, Maine, and had lived in Lawrence about twelve years. A monument marks his resting place. The monument was erected by the City Government.

The regiment quartered in Washington till May 5th, when it was ordered to the Relay House, where it remained till July 22d, the expiration of the three months for which it was called into action, and it was dismissed. The Lawrence companies were welcomed home with great enthusiasm, congratulatory speeches, a procession and other features characterizing the day.

The year following, 1862, when the government issued a call for nine months' men, the Sixth Regiment was again recruited to help fill the quota. Company I was organized from this city with A. L. Hamilton as captain, E. H. Ellenwood 1st lieutenant, and R. H. Barr 2d lieutenant. Upon the staff from this city was Melvin Beal, Lieut. Colonel. The regiment did duty on the Blackwater and were engaged in several fights. It was mustered out May 25th, 1862. The last active campaign of the Sixth was as one hundred days' men, and it was quite monotonous, duty Col. Beal was still Lieutenant Colonel. Company K was mustered from Lawrence, with E. J. Sherman as captain, Moulton Batchelder 1st lieutenant, and John D. Emerson 2d lieutenant. The time was spent mostly in forts.

In the 14th Infantry, commonly known as the Essex County regiment, Lawrence was represented by two companies, F and K. On the staff during the war, there were from this city, Lieut-Col. Levi P. Wright, Major Frank A. Rolfe, (killed) and Frank Davis. Company F was commanded by Captain Samuel Langmaid, J. W. Kimball 1st lieutenant, John H. Glover, 2d. Company K by Captain Frank A. Rolfe, Caleb Saunders, 1st lieutenant, William Preston, 2d. On the first of January, 1862, it was changed into the First Massachusetts Heavy Artillery. Early in April the regiment was required to furnish garrison for several forts in Virginia, and August 26th they received orders to participate in the battles of Bull Run, but did no fighting at that time. They lay on their arms one night. The regiment sub-

DANIEL F. DOLAN,

Wool Hat Finisher. Place of business, Methuen. House, 85 Cross St. A resident of Lawrence twenty-three years. Born in Ireland, March 19th, 1847; is not married, and is a Roman Catholic in his church connections. Served in the Common Council, from Ward IV, in 1874, and was president of the body during that year. Was elected commanding officer of Co. I., 6th Reg't M. V. M. in June 1877, and commissioned the following month. Is at present the Captain of said company.

sequently returned to garrison duty. In May 1864 the regiment marched to join the army of the Potomac, and was assigned to Tyler's division, Colonel Tannatt commanding. On the 19th, the regiment was in a severe engagement in which two officers were killed, fifteen wounded, fifty-three men killed, and two hundred and ninety-seven wounded, and twenty-seven reported missing. June 3d, occurred the battle of Cold Harbor, the regiment being engaged in charging on the enemy's works in the morning, and the repulse at night. In frequent engagements during the summer, it lost heavily. In February 1865, the regiment began active service. On the 25th of August, 1865, the regiment was discharged, having been in service four years, one month and twenty-one days.

In the 26th regiment Companys F and I were recruited in this city. Company F was commanded by Captain Annabel, with E. Caufy as 1st lieutenant, George E. Yerrington, 2d. Company I was commanded by Captain John Pickering, 1st lieutenant Charles E. Drew, and Badger 2d.

In the 41st Infantry, changed to Third Cavalry, was Company B. E. L. Noyes, captain, C. T. Batchelder, 1st lieutenant, Chas. Stone, 2d lieutenant. Colonel L. D. Sargent also belonged to this regiment.

Company C of the 40th regiment was mustered also from this city, with Stephen D. Stokes captain, Eugene J. Mason 1st lieutenant, J. F. Weare 2d lieutenant.

In the 17th regiment this city was represented by Company I, Thomas Weir captain, Michael Burns 1st lieutenant. The second lieutenant did not belong to this city.

One company of three years' men were also recruited from this city that joined the New York Mozart regiment.

In the nine months' regiments, two companies were raised in this city for the 4th regiment, B and H. B. was commanded by Captain

E. T. Colby, with Geo. S. Merrill as 1st lieutenant, and John K. Tarbox as 2d lieutenant. Company H, John R. Rollins captain, J. G. Abbott 1st lieutenant, and Hiram Robinson 2d.

In the ninety days men the eighth unattached company was commanded by Captain A. L. Hamilton, with E. H. Ellenwood as 1st, and Fred. G. Tyler as 2d lieutenant.

What the "boys" endured in the way of suffering and hardships while in the army of the rebellion will but a small part ever be told. Many were killed, many died of wounds and disease, and many others were diseased and maimed for life. The personal history of several of them would of itself make a volume. We will briefly follow the history of but one and from that the reader can glean something of the experience of many who took part in the whole campaign. Captain L. N. Duchesney whose portrait is in this book enlisted as a private in Company F, Sixth regiment, at the first call "to arms" and was with the regiment in its "march through Baltimore." Arriving at Washington he was detailed as telegraph operator. Came home and was mustered out August 2d, 1861. Enlisted as private in Company H, 1st Mass. Cavalry. November 22d, was promoted to corporal and shortly after to sergeant, and then to orderly; commissioned 2d lieutenant January 16th, 1863; 1st lieutenant February 16th, 1864. Mustered out April 3d, 1864. Was subsequently commissioned captain 1st battalion of 1st Mass. Cavalry, in the 26th New York Cavalry, March 1865, and was stationed on the frontier at Ogdensburg and Champlain. Since the war Captain Duchesney enlisted as private in Company C, 6th regiment, M. V. M., May 3d, 1871. 1st lieutenant, May 1871. Resigned and discharged Nov. 20th, 1872. Elected and commissioned Captain August 23d, 1873, and has held this position since that time.

The above tells only the bright side. But while in the army earning these promotions Captain Duchesney took active parts in the following battles. Fredericksburg, Chancellorville, Rapidan Station,

LAURENCE N. DUCHESNEY,

Inspector of Customs at the Boston Custom House. Residence, 46 Lowell St., Lawrence. Born in Canada, Sept., 1842. Came to this city in 1858. He was employed in the packing room at the Pacific Mills until the war of the rebellion broke out. For his army record see pages 172, 173 and 174 of this history. Capt. Duchesney has been commander of Needham Post, No. 39, G. A. R. His family consists of a wife and two children.

Rappahanock Bridge, Stevensburg, Brandy Station, Culpepper, Kelly's Ford, Popple Grove Church, Union Mills, Aldie, Secessionville, all in Virginia in the Army of the Potomac. He joined the department of the South and took part in the battles at French Brook, Raytown, Granville, and Chockee River, in East Tennessee.

At the last fight in Virginia he was taken prisoner of war June 17th, 1863, and taken to Richmond to Libby Prison. While here he was selected as a hostage and sentenced to be hung. Put into solitary confinement for sixty-nine days and nights, half starved, and expected every moment to be taken to the scaffold for execution. At the expiration of this time he was taken to Salisbury, N. C., and for three months with three others were under orders to be shot in retaliation for four bushwhackers hung by Burnside in Tennessee. When the authorities at Washington found out that they were thus sentenced they sent word to the "rebs" that if these men were shot the government would immediately shoot Gen. Fitzhugh Lee, a son of Gen. Winder, and two other noted Southerners who were then prisoners of war held by the U. S. government. This caused the sentence to be deferred and finally abandoned. He was then taken to be carried to Danville, but while on the way he escaped by jumping from the cars while in motion about ten o'clock at night. This was twelve miles from Greensboro'. Three others escaped at the same time, Captain E. M. Driscoll, Third Ohio Infantry, Lieut. Quimby, Ninth New Hampshire, and Sergeant Hayes of this city. The latter was captured and taken back. These other three wended their way due westward, travelling nights and stealing or begging scanty supplies to sustain life as the case might be, going 1500 miles through the enemy's country, arriving at Knoxville, Tennessee, January 13th, 1864. While passing through the mountains Captain Duchesney joined himself for a while with bushwhackers and finally with Col. Kirk's North Carolina Cavalry, all of whom were engaged in guerrilla warfare against the Secessionists. Upon arriving at Knoxville he reported to General Green, Provost Marshal, and was at once by order of Secretary Stanton sent to Washington and mustered out of service, his time having expired.

THE MILITIA.

The headquarters of the Sixth Regiment Massachusetts Volunteer Militia are in this city. Colonel Beal, the commander at the first call for soldiers to put down the rebellion, was a member of the State Militia, 2d Lieutenant of Company F, Sixth Regiment. On the 6th of May, same year, he was commissioned Captain. When the regiment was recruited for nine months service in 1862 he was commissioned Lieutenant Colonel, serving in this capacity during this enlistment, and the subsequent 100 days' service. January 30th, 1863, had his horse killed at his side in the battle on the Blackwater, and also received honorable mention for bravery. Since the close of the war Colonel Beal has been the commander of the Sixth Regiment, M. V. M. Company I, Captain Daniel F. Dolan, and Company K, Captain L. N. Duchesney, of this regiment are located here. Major Smith M. Decker, and Adjutant Charles H. Littlefield and paymaster L. G. Holt of the Staff also belong to Lawrence.

TIMOTHY DACEY,

Hotel Keeper, of firm of T. Dacey & Co., proprietors of Boston Hotel, 200 Essex St. Has been in Lawrence since early childhood. Born in Clonakilty, Cork Co., Ireland, 1837. Was a member of the common council for 1871–2, a member of the police force in 1868, and a member of the house of representatives, 1877. Captain Dacey was formerly prominently connected with the Fenian movement, and was sent in 1865 by the Lawrence Fenian Club to England, where he was arrested soon after his arrival. He was released and subsequently arrested and rescued, several of his rescuers being hung for the offence. Enlisted in Co. I, 9th Mass. Reg't, June, 1861; promoted to sergeant June, 1861, 2nd lieutenant, Sept., 1862, 1st lieutenant, April, 1863. Was wounded in the "Battle of the Wilderness," May, 1864. Mustered out June, 1864. Enlisted in Co. I, 6th Reg't, M. V. M., Jan. 1871; was elected captain in February, same year; resigned June, 1877.

XVII.

THE CITY MISSION—CATHOLIC SOCIETIES, NEWSPAPERS, ETC.

LAWRENCE CITY MISSION.

In a new city like this, the philanthropic people soon saw the need of caring for a certain class, unfortunately destitute, who were not and ought not to be classed paupers. Rev. Mr. Harrington of the Unitarian church was the first to apply this principle, and in the years 1852–3 solicited contributions throughout the parish and acted himself as distributing agent. This worked so well that on the 29th day of December, 1854, an assembly was convened agreeably to call and an association organized called the "Lawrence Provident Association." The officers elected were, President, John C. Hoadley; Vice Presidents, George Packard and J. D. Herrick; Treasurer, W. D. Lamb; Secretary, Richard H. Rust, who was at that time pastor of the Haverhill street M. E. church. The plan of the work was to raise funds by contributions and distribute them through ward committees, three from each ward being chosen for that purpose. Monthly meetings were held and reports made on the condition of the work. January 6th, 1857, George P. Wilson was elected general agent and treasurer, but declined the position at that time owing to other engagements, and Henry Withington was chosen in his stead.

At the annual meeting in October, 1858, Dr. Packard was elected President, N. P. Houghton Secretary, and George P. Wilson General Agent and Treasurer, at a salary of $600 per annum. At length it was thought that an organization more comprehensive would better serve the purposes of the people, and in accordance with the following vote delegates were chosen :

Voted, That a committee of two from each religious society be invited to meet in convention with a committee of two from the Provident Association to take into consideration the subject of establishing a City Mission:

Provident Association.—George Packard, William D. Lamb.
Grace Church.—James Payne, B. F. Watson.
Lawrence Street Church.—Benjamin Coolidge, Chas. H. Bigelow.
Central Church.—Daniel Tenney, John Fallon.
Universalist Church.—Robert Stere, Artemas Harmon.
Unitarian Church.—Charles S. Storrow, H. K. Oliver.
Free Baptist Church.—E. M. Tappan, Simeon Briggs.
First Baptist Church.—S. C. Woodward, A. J. French.
Presbyterian Church.—John McKay, Mr. Daylish.
First Methodist Church.—Amasa Bryant, N. Ambrose.
Garden Street Church.—W. F. Evans, David Ambrose.
Common Street Presbyterian.—J. Hudson, John Clayton.
Spiritualist.—W. R. Wason, J. C. Bowker.

The delegates were convened March 23d, 1859, and the Lawrence City Mission organized. Dr. Packard was chosen President, and Rev. George P. Wilson Missionary. The organization has since continued, managed by a board of advice elected and constituted similar to the original delegates. Through this agency some $2,500 in money and clothing has been collected and distributed annually. The salary of the Missionary has been raised by the corporations outside of this fund.

CHARLES URBANE DUNNING,

City Missionary, Chaplain at the Jail and House of Correction, and clergyman of the Methodist faith. Mission office, 205 Essex Street; residence, 89 Newbury Street. Was for three years pastor the Garden St. M. E. Church—1866–9. City Missionary and Chaplain at the Jail since 1872. Born at Ithica, Tompkins Co., N. Y., July, 1829. Married Harriet Frances Batchelder, 1858; has three children. (For history of early life and preparation for life-work see history of City Mission in this book.) Mr. Dunning has been stationed for pastoral work in New Hampshire as follows: East Sanbornton, (now East Tilton,) 1854; Chester, 1855; Bethlehem and Carroll, 1856; North Haverhill, 1858; Haverhill, 1858–9; Enfield, 1860; East Canaan, 1862-6; three years in this city and three years at Dover, returning from that place to Lawrence.

Rev. George P. Wilson than whom the poor of the city never had a firmer friend, continued to hold the office of Missionary till April, 1872, when he resigned to accept a position in the Methodist Conference, stationed at South Boston. A little more than a year from that time, July 10th, 1873, he sickened and died. His remains were brought here for interment, the funeral being held in the Garden street church. He was buried in Bellevue Cemetery, a beautiful monument on the eastern slope marking his resting place.

At the same meeting of the resignation of Mr. Wilson, the board elected as his successor Rev. C. U. Dunning the present incumbent. Mr. Dunning came from Exeter, though he was no stranger, having been previously stationed over the Garden street church. He was peculiarly fitted for the position—reared in a Christian home in Utica, New York, first studying law and afterwards preparing for the ministry. He was ordained in 1858 and had been appointed spiritual guide over eight different Methodist churches before accepting the position of Missionary.

CATHOLIC SOCIETIES.

Connected with the Catholic churches of the city are several organizations for the promotion of temperance, mutual relief and charity. These have a numerous membership and usually on St. Patricks day they turn out in procession and make a very creditable display. The oldest of these is the Irish Catholic Benevolent Society, organized October 15, 1863. As its name implies its object is mutual charity and the disbursements for this object are upwards of one thousand dollars annually.

The Father Mathew Total Abstinence Society is the largest society of its nature in Essex County. It was organized in 1869. Its president is Joseph T. Nichols.

There are two lodges of the Ancient Order of Hibernians, Nos. 1 and 8. These are beneficial organizations and weekly sick benefits of $5.00 per week are paid. The president of No. 1 is John O'Keefe and No. 8, John T. O'Connor.

The Knights of St. Patrick embrace some of the most wealthy and cultured of the Catholic faith in the city. They have a handsome uniform and number about 100 members. The commander is Patrick Ford, treasurer Wm. H. Keefe.

NEWSPAPERS.

To write at length the history of the newspapers of the city would make an interesting chapter to those familiar with the business, but to the average reader it would be exceedingly dull. The career of none has been brilliant. All the early ventures were failures, and of the last decade their growth has only corresponded with the growth of the city. Considering the capital and brains required in their production no paper in Lawrence could be said to be a paying investment. But newspapers are not made, they grow. And some of those in this city are destined in the course of time to be powerful metropolitan sheets.

J. F. C. Hayes was the man who inaugurated the newspaper enterprise here. Early in 1846 he came to this city and set up a printing press in a partially completed block on Broadway. He soon threw out a little weekly sheet called the Merrimac Courier, afterwards called the Lawrence Weekly and Tri-Weekly Courier. He continued them for a few years and before they expired in 1862, they had been under the guiding hands of John A. Goodwin, Homer A. Cook, and Nathaniel Ambrose. They were finally merged into a paper called the Daily Journal, but soon expired. In January 1847, the Weekly Messenger, by Brown & Beckett, was transferred from Exeter, N. H., but lived only about two years. Then followed the Herald and the Vanguard, both Democratic papers; the latter was published by Fabyan & Douglas, the former by Amos H. Sampson. After a time the Vanguard was changed to the Sentinel, which still continues under the management of Abiel Morrison & Son. In 1854 the Home Review was started by J. F. C. Hayes, afterwards transferred to Frank Leath, but lived only a few months. In 1855 Geo. W. Sargent and A. S. Bunker began the Lawrence American as a Know Nothing organ. Mr. Bunker soon sold out to Mr. Sargent for twenty-five dollars; and Mr. Sargent was soon succeeded by Geo. S. Merrill, the present proprietor. In 1861 Dockham & Place began a daily paper, but it did not have an existence long enough to be worthy of the name of a daily paper.

In 1867 the Essex Eagle was started by Merrill & Wadsworth, Mr. Merrill soon retiring, and has of late been local editor of the Sentinel, Mr. Wadsworth continued on, starting the Daily Eagle from the same office, July 20, 1868. In 1873 he sold both papers to Hammon Reed, the present owner, Mr. Wadsworth still continuing with the paper. The Daily Eagle is the oldest daily in the city, the Daily American being issued the next evening.

The Lawrence Journal, weekly, was started by Robert Bower as a labor organ in 1871, but was sold in 1877 to Patrick Sweeney, the present proprietor. The only papers in Lawrence to-day are two dailies, the Eagle and the American, and four weeklies, the Eagle, American, Sentinel, and Journal.

HORACE A. WADSWORTH,

The compiler of this book and pioneer of sucessful daily journalism in Lawrence. Office, 307 Essex Street; house 65 Tremont Street. Born in Milford, N. H., 1837. Came to this city in 1866. Started the ESSEX WEEKLY EAGLE, 1867; LAWRENCE DAILY EAGLE, 1868, and is still connected with the office. Has a wife and three children. Attends Lawrence Street Congregational Church.

CONTENTS.

ILLUSTRATIONS AND PORTRAITS.

www.ingramcontent.com/pod-product-compliance
Lightning Source LLC
Chambersburg PA
CBHW021218270326
41929CB00010B/1179

* 9 7 8 3 7 4 4 6 9 2 5 8 8 *